Veloce Classic Reprint Series

MOTO GUZZI

SPORT & LE MANS BIBLE

V7 SPORT, 750S & S3, 850 LE MANS, 850 LE MANS II & III, 1000 LE MANS IV & V

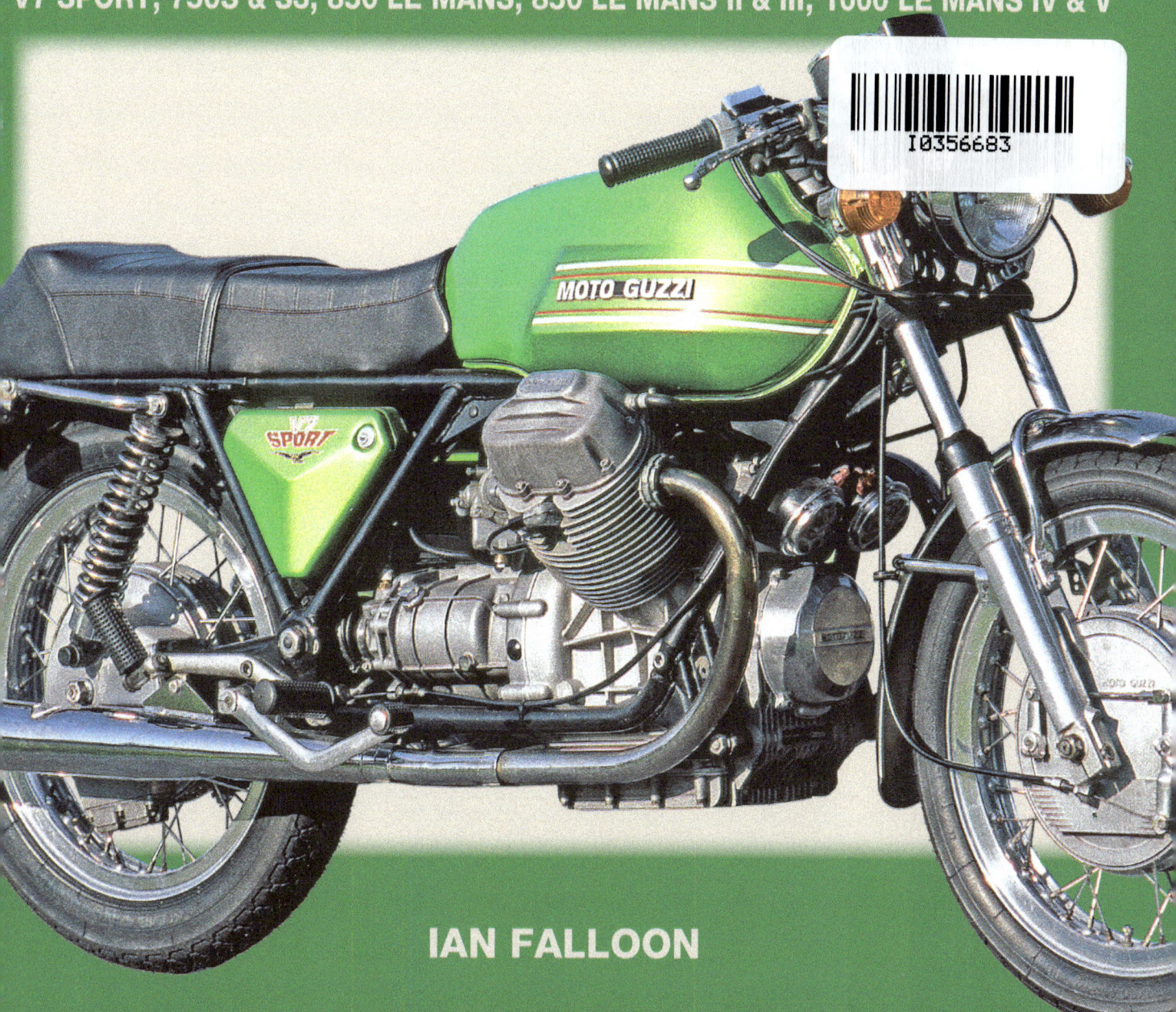

IAN FALLOON

First published April 2007 by Veloce, an imprint of David and Charles Limited. Tel +44 (0)1305 260068 / e-mail info@veloce.co.uk / web www.veloce.co.uk.
Reprinted January 2011. This classic edition printed March 2017, reprinted 2025.

ISBN: 9781787110953

© 2007, 2011 and 2017 & 2025 Ian Falloon and David and Charles. All rights reserved. With the exception of quoting brief passages for the purpose of review, no part of this publication may be recorded, transmitted or transmitted by any means, including photocopying, without the written permission of David and Charles Limited.
Throughout this book logos, model names and designations, etc, have been used for the purposes of identification, illustration and decoration. Such names are the property of the trademark holder as this is not an official publication. Readers with ideas for automotive books, or books on other transport or related hobby subjects, are invited to write to the editorial director of Veloce at the above email address. British Library Cataloguing in Publication Data – A catalogue record for this book is available from the British Library. Design and DTP by Veloce.

Contents

Introduction & acknowledgements 4

1 Moto Guzzi motorcycles before the V7 Sport.. 6
2 200kph & 200kg: the V7 Sport (1971-73) 17
3 De Tomaso style: 750 S & 750 S3 46
4 Style with speed: the 850 Le Mans (1975-78).. 59
5 Wind tunnel design: the Le Mans II & CX 100.. 75
6 Square heads.. 86
7 End of the line: Le Mans 1000... 97
8 Racing the V7 Sport & Le Mans. 125

Appendix – Specifications & production figures... 145
Index.. ... ... .159

Introduction & acknowledgements

Until 1958 Moto Guzzi always had a strong sporting and competition bias. Prior to the outbreak of World War II, Moto Guzzi was one of the leading marques on European racing circuits, and when racing resumed after the war Moto Guzzi remained at the forefront. During the 1960s Moto Guzzi barely managed to stay alive but its fortunes improved after 1967 with the release of the V7. This large touring machine seemed an unlikely basis for a sporting motorcycle, but when Lino Tonti and Luciano Gazzola joined Moto Guzzi, they brought with them the necessary knowledge and enthusiasm to create the V7 Sport.

In the early 1970s the motorcycle market moved beyond basic transportation to that of recreation. As buyers demanded more performance, this could only be satisfied by motorcycles with a capacity of at least 750cc: 750cc also happened to be the capacity established for new, production-based racing classes and, with this in mind, Tonti managed to transform the large V7 into one of the most beautiful and functional 750cc sporting motorcycles of all time – the V7 Sport Telaio Rosso. In 1971 the V7 Sport was one of the most expensive and exotic motorcycles available, albeit in limited quantities, and when it went into regular production in 1972, gave class-leading performance. Today, the V7 Sport is acknowledged as one of the classic motorcycles of the early Superbike era.

The purchase of Moto Guzzi by Alessandro de Tomaso at the end of 1972 almost signified the end of the sporting Moto Guzzi V-twin, but it survived and prospered, the V7 Sport evolving into the 750 S and S3, while, from the racing program, came another landmark model: the 850 Le Mans. Combining style and function more successfully than almost any motorcycle of the 1970s, the 850 Le Mans established a sporting lineage that would last 17 years.

Eventually, time caught up with the Le Mans. The air-cooled, two-valve engine could no longer meet increasing emission regulations, and the motorcycle world moved beyond 18-inch wheels and twin rear shock absorbers. But the model's appeal remained, and – even at the end – the Le Mans was an uncomplicated, easy-to-live-with sporting motorcycle that continues to command a strong following.

This book covers the Tonti-frame sporting Moto Guzzi twins from 1971 until 1993, including the final retro 1000 S. I have been fortunate to be able to draw on the unrivalled knowledge of Ivar de Gier, whose family has been deeply involved with Moto Guzzi for three generations. Ivar proofread the text, contributed considerable new information, and provided many period photographs. As Ivar shared with me many of his conversations with Lino Tonti and Luciani Gazzola over the ten year period before Tonti died, there is considerable previously unpublished material. Without Ivar's contribution this book would also be a lot less accurate. My contribution extended to a study of as many individual machines as possible over a thirty year period, plus an analysis of official spare parts manuals and workshop manuals. Each model has been broken down into a specific type and production period. With limited information available from Moto Guzzi there may well be inaccuracies; hopefully, these will be minimal. Intended as an historical analysis and description of the evolution of the Tonti-frame sporting twin, period photographs, or those of original condition machines, mean the book is also a guide to originality.

My own involvement with Moto Guzzi goes back to 1973, when I dreamed of owning a V7 Sport. I had to wait until 1977 to briefly own an 850 Le Mans, eventually purchasing a 1973 V7 Sport in 1999. These are classic motorcycles that still provide a wonderful riding experience, and are just as beautiful at rest as they are on the move.

Writing this book has been a passionate exercise, and there are many enthusiasts who have helped along the way. Special thanks for the use of photos must go to Moto Guzzi, Ivar de Gier, Jeremy Bowdler of *Two Wheels* magazine, and David Edwards of *Cycle World* magazine. Others who contributed with pictures and information include Hans Smid and Roy Kidney. Hans Smid and Marnix van der Schalk allowed the use of their perfect Le Mans for photography, whilst Mike Harper provided discount workshop, owners' manuals, and parts lists. I am also extremely fortunate to have the ongoing support of my wife, Miriam, and sons, Ben and Tim, which allows me to undertake these demanding projects.

Ian Falloon
Kew, Australia

Moto Guzzi motorcycles before the V7 Sport

When the V7 Sport appeared in 1971, it re-established a racing and sporting tradition that had been absent from Moto Guzzi for nearly fifteen years. Prior to 1958, Moto Guzzi built its reputation on racing success, culminating in an astonishing record of 14 World Championships, 47 Italian Championships, and 3329 racing victories between 1921 and 1957. This racing glory resulted in some of the finest sporting motorcycles of the pre-war and immediate post-war period, and the V7 Sport continued this tradition.

The Moto Guzzi story began in the Italian air force during World War I when Carlo Guzzi, a 29-year-old mechanic, teamed up with two pilots, Giorgio Parodi and Giovanni Ravelli, to build a motorcycle. Although Ravelli died in an aircraft accident shortly after the end of the war, Guzzi and Parodi pursued their dream. Parodi, from a wealthy family of shipowners, was to provide the capital, and Guzzi the engineering expertise. Ravelli's memory endured in the shape of the air force flying eagle symbol used.

During 1920, in a workshop at the family home in Tonzanico (later known as Mandello del Lario), on the shore of Lake Como, north of Milan, Carlo Guzzi produced the first Moto Guzzi, the 'GP' (Guzzi-Parodi), and with it established an independent design philosophy that characterised Moto Guzzi motorcycles. The GP was powered by a four-valve, horizontal, 500cc, single cylinder overhead camshaft engine, with a unit three-speed gearbox and external flywheel. Looking for financial backing, Giorgio approached his father, Emanuelle Vittorio Parodi, who had the GP transported to a friend, an

Carlo Guzzi was the engineering impetus behind the creation of Moto Guzzi and was involved with the company until his death in 1964. (Courtesy Moto Guzzi)

engineering professor in Barcelona. After a thorough examination the professor sent a letter of approval to Emanuelle. The GP went back to Genoa and, eventually, Tonzanico. This positive reaction led Parodi to establish the Società Anomina Moto Guzzi in Genoa in March 1921, with himself as president. Although the company was named after Carlo Guzzi, Emanuelle retained the company shares, paying Carlo a royalty for each machine produced. In 1921 the GP was tested by *The Motor Cycle* magazine, the first test of a Moto Guzzi in the English press.

Soon after the company was established, the first Moto Guzzi motorcycle, the Normale, entered production. Designed earlier by Carlo, he was assisted and influenced by his brother, Giuseppe, who wanted to ensure the design was a success, and that it was. By the end of 1921 the Normale was winning races, this success leading to the two-valve racing C2V in 1923, and four-valve C4V in 1924 (closely derived from the GP). Soon the Sport – with a more powerful engine and chassis similar to the C2V – replaced the Normale. The Sport formed the basis of the production line-up until 1928, with the racing C2V and C4V also available, as was a sidecar version of the Sport.

During this period the racing programme continued to expand, and the most significant victory was in the first Championship of Europe, held at Monza on 7 September 1924. Guido Mentasti, on a C4V, beat the field consisting of the works Sunbeam, Norton, Saroléa, and Peugeot; Moto Guzzi was no longer an obscure Italian motorcycle manufacturer. For 1926, Carlo Guzzi created a new competition machine, the TT250, which became one of the

Moto Guzzi's first production model was the Normale of 1921. This 500cc single was extremely advanced and instigated a design philosophy independent of tradition which continues today.

most successful racing motorcycles of the era. While small numbers of racing 500s (the 4VTT and 4VSS) were also made available to privateers, the production line continued to turn out 500cc Sports. In 1928 Giuseppe Guzzi also produced a sprung frame for the Sport, creating the advanced – but not particularly popular – GT. The Sport evolved into the Sport 14 in 1929 and the Sport 15 in 1931, while the sprung frame GT became the GT 16.

While many motorcycle manufacturers suffered in the wake of the 1929 Wall Street Crash, Moto Guzzi prospered, as Mussolini and his Fascist government

One of the most spectacular racing Moto Guzzis of the 1930s was the 500cc Bicilindrica. After the Second World War it was resurrected and raced virtually unchanged. This is how it appeared in 1947, almost as Stanley Woods rode it to victory in the 1935 Senior TT. (Courtesy Moto Guzzi)

motor sport to be an important propaganda tool. Considerable resources were expended in the creation of an (unsuccessful) supercharged, 500cc, four-cylinder racer in 1931, followed by an equally ambitious production three-cylinder touring machine. But Guzzi's most successful models continued to be singles, in particular the racing 250, a new range of motoleggere, or lightweight motorcycle, and the military GT 17, the first of a long line built for specific military application.

Desperately needing a competitive 500 in the wake of the failure of the racing four-cylinder, Carlo Guzzi built a twin out of two SS250 singles. This was the Bicilindrica, a design that lasted from 1933 until 1951, and successfully blended the balance between horsepower and agility. In the design of the Bicilindrica, Carlo Guzzi retained the horizontal cylinder of the SS250, and placed another cylinder 120 degrees behind it. Both featured a single overhead camshaft driven by a shaft and bevel gears, and, in the hands of the brilliant rider, Omobono Tenni, spearheaded Moto Guzzi's 500cc racing programme for nearly twenty years.

The production 500cc, single cylinder engine was also completely redesigned for 1934, and was named the 'V'. While retaining the distinctive horizontal cylinder and external flywheel, valve layout included two overhead valves operated by pushrods and rockers with external hairpin springs. The cylinder head initially featured twin exhaust ports, the gearbox was four-speed, and Guzzi's design formed the basis of all later Guzzi 500 singles, including the magnificent Condor, Dondolino, and Gambalunga competition machines.

For 1935 the official Guzzi 250 and 500cc racers received a sprung frame. Veteran Isle of Man specialist, Stanley Woods, claimed Guzzi victories in the Lightweight and Senior TTs, a landmark victory, signalling the end of the dominance of British rigid frame singles in the blue-ribbon 500cc class. At the same time, Moto Guzzi grew in status to a world class motorcycle manufacturer. The Italian invasion of Ethiopia curtailed competition involvement during 1936, but Moto Guzzi was back at the Isle of Man in 1937, Tenni winning the Lightweight TT.

In the years prior to the outbreak of World War II, Guzzi produced a supercharged 250 racer, and in 1939 released two new catalogue racers: the 500cc Condor and 250cc Albatros. All were immediately successful, and so advanced that they were resurrected after the war. In 1940 Guzzi unveiled a machine – the Tre Cilindri 500 – that could have made Guzzi unbeatable in the 500cc class if war hadn't intervened. Developed in response to the supercharged Gilera, BMW, and NSU, Guzzi's supercharged 500 triple arrived too late ...

The 250cc Albatros was a catalogued racing machine that could be purchased by privateers. Produced from 1938, it, too, was resurrected in 1946 and was extremely successful. This is a post-war example. (Courtesy Roy Kidney)

Moto Guzzi motorcycles before the V7 Sport

The final Bicilindrica was the 1951 version, now incorporating an aerodynamically sculptured fuel tank.

From 1940 Moto Guzzi was almost totally committed to the production of military motorcycles, in particular the Alce, Trialce, and Motocarri 500U. Situated away from major industrial centres, when normal manufacture resumed late in 1945, the company was ready to take on the world in providing cheap transportation, which provided the resources to allow Moto Guzzi to become a major force in motorcycle road racing.

Post-war success

In 1942, while Giorgio Parodi was serving in the Italian forces, his brother, Enrico, assumed control of the company. When Giorgio was forced to retire from the company through injury, Enrico continued as manager, and instigated a fresh approach. He saw the demand for basic transportation in Italy in the immediate post-war period, and under his direction Moto Guzzi became a mass producer of small motorcycles. Led by the two-stroke Motoleggera 65, and the later, scooter-like Galletto, by 1950 Moto Guzzi was producing more than 30,000 motorcycles a year. Now one of the largest motorcycle manufacturers in the world, the revenue generated from the sales of mass produced, lightweight motorcycles enabled Moto Guzzi to expand its racing programme, and create sophisticated racing prototypes. The traditional four-stroke single was also revived during this period. The machines produced – the 250cc Airone, and 500cc Astore and Falcone – had long and distinguished production runs, and while the number produced was relatively small, they have come to symbolise the production Moto Guzzi during the 1950s. The Falcone continued until 1968, still remarkably similar to its 1920s and 1930s ancestors, before it was updated to the Nuovo Falcone. During the 1950s, smaller capacity, four-stroke singles were also produced in reasonable numbers, headed by Carlo Guzzi's final design, the 175cc, overhead camshaft Lodola (Skylark). The Lodola evolved into a Sport for 1958, and by 1959 had grown to 235cc (now with pushrods) to replace the ageing Airone.

Whilst the production line at Mandello was expanded to include the Motoleggera, Moto Guzzi resurrected some of the pre-war racers, adapting them for new, post-war regulations. A ban on supercharging left the door open for the return of the pre-war Bicilindrica, and Guzzi also decided to develop the pre-war single cylinder Albatros and Condor. The Condor evolved into the superb Dondolino (rocking chair) and Gambalunga (long-leg), with a longer stroke engine. Renowned for its ruggedness and strength, the Dondolino's forte was long distance events like the Milano-Taranto road race, which it won from 1950 until 1953. The Gambalunga was a factory racer, developed by the great engineer, Giulio Cesare Carcano, with a leading link front fork.

As it was optimistic to expect the pushrod, overhead valve, single cylinder Gambalunga to be competitive in 500cc racing, Moto Guzzi revived the Bicilindrica. Updated Bicilindricas went on to win the 1947 and 1948 Italian Championships, and it was developed until 1951. Although the Bicilindrica was moderately successful, the modernized Albatros and subsequent Gambalunghino were far more eficacious. At the Isle of Man in 1947, Manliff Barrington rode an Albatros to victory in the Lightweight TT, Maurice Cann repeating this in 1948. When the World Championships for motorcycles were created in 1949, Moto Guzzi was better prepared than other manufacturers, particularly in the 250cc class.

For the 1949 season, Moto Guzzi created the 250cc Gambalunghino; essentially an Albatros engine in a Gambalunga chassis with leading link front suspension. While not the fastest machine, the Gambalunghino's superior reliability allowed rider, Ruffo, to win the World Championship. Considering the compact horizontal 250cc single, with its geared primary drive and external flywheel, first appeared in 1926, this success was remarkable.

The 250 was outclassed during 1950, but further development of the venerable single overhead camshaft Gambalunghino for 1951 saw Ruffo again win the 250cc World Championship. Commissioning of the wind tunnel for 1952 meant that aerodynamics began to play as important a role as engine development. Lower and narrower, the Gambalunghino proved virtually unbeatable, with Enrico Lorenzetti winning the 1952 world title from Fergus Anderson.

Buoyant from the sale of Guzzinos, for 1953 Moto Guzzi decided to build a replacement for the Bicilindrica to contest the 500cc category. Another original and unique design, the inline 500 four stunned the world – but was a disaster. Designed by Rome-based engineer, Carlo Gianini, in order to reduce frontal area the 500 was a longitudinal, water-cooled, four-cylinder with shaft final drive that closely followed automotive practice. Unfortunately, the disadvantages of the inline four outweighed the advantages. The torque reaction from the crankshaft caused problems, and the engine speed clutch made gear changing difficult. While it occasionally showed bursts of speed, the four was extremely unreliable and difficult to ride. In many respects the 500 four was extremely advanced, with features that did appear on later Moto Guzzis. As on the later V7, the shaft was located inside the swingarm, and braking was by a linked system. The engine was also fuel injected.

It was in the 350cc class that Guzzi had most success during 1953, a class that it dominated until 1957. After several years of testing various prototypes, Carcano finally discovered the right formula. Earlier 350s were simply a bored and stroked Gambalunghino, and this was initially what Fergus Anderson persuaded Carcano to do late in 1952. Anderson wanted to compete against the Nortons and AJSs, traditional class leaders, and the engine was enlarged to 317cc, the maximum possible. Eventually, the engine cases were redesigned to allow for 345cc, and Anderson won the World Championship.

Australian rider, Ken Kavanagh, joined the team for 1954 alongside Anderson, Lorenzetti, Montanari and Ruffo. This year saw the first dustbin fairings developed with the aid of the wind tunnel, and a new single overhead camshaft, 500cc single developed from the Gambalunghino. Light and overstressed, it proved unreliable and, despite excellent aerodynamics, was never a match for the MV Agusta and Gilera fours.

Replacing the Albatros in 1949 was the Gambalunghino (little long leg) with leading link front suspension. This machine was also incredibly successful, Ruffo winning the 1949 and 1951 250cc World Championships on it.

Moto Guzzi motorcycles before the V7 Sport

Creation of the astonishing 500cc V8 was indicative of the impressive resources that Moto Guzzi had available in the mid-1950s, and the brilliance of the designer, Carcano.

As it was the 350cc Championship that Guzzi was defending, most development went into this machine. The engine now featured a double overhead camshaft, and enclosed valve gear with single coil valve springs. There was a new trellis frame, and fuel was initially carried in pannier tanks on each side of the dustbin fairing. Although the season started indifferently, Anderson did retain the World Championship.

Anderson retired from racing to manage the team during 1955, and Duilio Agostini and Dickie Dale joined Kavanagh as works riders. Although Enrico Parodi was concerned about the cost of running the racing programme, he did sanction development of one of the most amazing racing Moto Guzzis, the V8. More than any other design the V8 demonstrates the resources and technical expertise available to Moto Guzzi during the mid-1950s. Carcano was allowed a free hand, and the result was an engine too advanced for the frame and tyre technology of the day.

The water-cooled, 90 degree V8 was an incredible design, with many unusual features. The crankcase consisted of a one-piece magnesium casting mounted transversely across the frame, initially incorporating a 6-speed gearbox. The valves were operated by double overhead camshafts driven by straight-cut gears, and initial power was 68 horsepower at 12,000rpm. The frame was a duplex cradle, with leading link forks, the swingarm pivoting from the rear of the engine. Total weight was only 150kg, and the V8 was developed so quickly it raced at a few events during 1955.

The Grand Prix 350 for 1955 was powered by a new short-stroke engine; to save weight Carcano wouldn't allow the electron fairings to be painted in anything more than anti-corrosive green protective paint, which came to distinguish the racing Moto Guzzis. 1955 was a vintage year in the 350cc World Championship as Moto Guzzi won every race, and Bill Lomas the championship, earning him a two-year works contract.

Development of the V8 continued for 1956, and while it impressed everyone with its speed it was unreliable. The amazing single continued to dominate in the 350cc class, Kavanagh winning the Junior TT at the Isle of Man, and Lomas his second World Championship. The final year for an official racing team was 1957. The V8 finally began to win races, notably in the hands of Dickie Dale who won the Easter Imola Gold Cup. And despite injuries to Lomas and Dale later in the season, another 350cc World Championship was secured by new recruit, Australian Keith Campbell. The success of the 350cc single in the wake of increased opposition from more powerful, four-cylinder machines was a vindication of Carcano's philosophy of achieving more through less. Carcano's obsession with weight saving, weight distribution, and excellent aerodynamics rewarded Moto Guzzi with two 250cc and five 350cc World Championships.

At the end of September 1957 Moto Guzzi, along with Gilera and Mondial, announced its withdrawal from Grand Prix racing. While racing success had been a wonderful advertising exercise, during 1957 there was a severe downturn in worldwide motorcycle sales. Many manufacturers were finding the cost of racing difficult to justify, including Moto Guzzi.

The V7

Withdrawal from racing coincided with an era of decline for Moto Guzzi. Although responsible for some brilliant initiatives, Enrico Parodi lost direction and foresight, failing to respond to the general downturn in motorcycle sales. He underestimated the significance of the Fiat 500 in the Italian market for mass transportation: when prosperity arrived in the mid-1960s, the Italian consumer deserted the basic motorcycle for a car. Parodi put his faith in the small, two-stroke Dingo, but this was misguided. There were also other problems facing the company. Much of the plant and machinery was out of date, as was the management and marketing. The crisis deepened and by 1966 Parodi's financial backing was lost and the company went into receivership.

Prior to this crisis, development of new ideas continued. Immediately after withdrawing from racing Carcano began designing a sporting cylinder head for his BMW sports car. He had worked for BMW (and NSU) during World War II but his work on the BMW, while employed by Moto Guzzi, met with disparagement. BMW was regarded as a competitor so Carcano turned his attention to his other automotive interest, the Fiat Topolino.

Carcano believed it would be fun to build a Topolino capable of 140kph (87mph) and, as he did not consider the Fiat engine suitable for tuning, began designing a new V-twin engine. The first sketches appeared later that year and work continued during 1958, initially as an academic exercise. Built initially in 1959 for a Fiat car as a 500, then 650cc unit, this Fiat engine can be considered the predecessor of the V7 that would eventually power the V7 Sport and Le Mans. With forced air cooling and twin carburettors, it produced 34 horsepower, enough to propel the tiny car to Carcano's target speed of 140kph (87mph).

Carcano completed the design, built an engine in the Guzzi factory, and installed it in his own Topolino. In an interview with Ivar de Gier in 2005, Carcano said: "That car quickly became my favourite form of transportation. Once, when coming home from Milan, I passed an Alfa Romeo sportscar driven by a motoring journalist. The journalist, amazed at my speed, suspected it was a Fiat prototype. He traced the license tag, discovered the car ownership, and assumed that Moto Guzzi was developing a new engine for Fiat. But this was not true. Fiat asked Guzzi to provide an engine for the Fiat 500 but in the end chose an Abarth design".

The Fiat engine was shelved until the V7 project. Carcano told Ivar he was reluctant to use this engine for a motorcycle, and would

MOTO GUZZI MOTORCYCLES BEFORE THE V7 SPORT

have preferred to do many things differently. Although the Fiat project was abandoned, many of the design characteristics continued on the unsuccessful 3x3 Autoveicolo da Montagna (mechanical mule) that was developed in parallel. The 3x3 engine was designed by Antonio Micucci and not Carcano, and, apart from its 90 degree, V-twin layout, shared little with the eventual V7: the crankcases, displacement, cylinder head and lubrication system were all different.

It was the tender for a new police motorcycle to replace the Falcone that would give a more satisfactory outcome for Carcano's V-twin. Moto Guzzi had long been a primary supplier of Italian police and military vehicles, so it was with some surprise that a tender for a new motorcycle was announced early in 1963. It was vital for Moto Guzzi's survival that it secured the tender, and in May 1963 Carcano and Todero – assisted by Micucci and Soldavini – began serious work on the project. Requirements included a service life of 100,000 kilometres, and whilst other Italian manufacturers (Benelli, Ducati, Gilera, and Laverda) favoured parallel twins, Carcano decided to resurrect his earlier Fiat 90 degree, V-twin design. Todero completed early drawings by the end of May, and by November 1964 the first prototype was ready, just in time for Carlo Guzzi to see it before he died. Testing continued throughout 1965, and a civilian version was displayed at the Milan Show in November 1965; Moto Guzzi won the police contract.

The designation V7 derived from the V layout and 700cc engine (which was cleverly designed to provided long-term reliability and easy servicing). A 90 degree, V-twin, all-alloy design, like the earlier Fiat and 3x3 the V7 had pushrod operated overhead valves with the camshaft situated between the cylinders, driven by helical gears from the crankshaft. Unlike most motorcycle engines of the time, the one-piece steel crankshaft used plain big-end and two plain main bearings. Replacement of the lower end bearings could be achieved without removing the engine from the frame.

With the V7, Moto Guzzi embarked on the era of the big-twin that continues to sustain the company today. (Courtesy Moto Guzzi)

Many of the design features went unchanged throughout the entire production life of the engine: the con-rod length of 140mm; the 22mm gudgeon, and 44mm crankpin. The plain bearings required a high pressure lubrication system, with three litres of oil contained in a detachable sump underneath the engine. Unlike the 3x3 that had no oil filtration, the V7 included wire gauze located at the bottom of the crankcase directly connected to the oil pump. Bore and stroke of the first version was 80x70mm, giving a displacement of 703.717cc. The cylinder bores were chrome-plated, and the two overhead valves were set at an included angle of 70 degrees. Carburation was via two Dell'Orto SS1 29mm carburettors; ignition by an automotive-type Marelli S 123A distributor, driven off the rear of the camshaft, and power was 50 horsepower at 6300rpm.

The clutch and final drive followed automotive rather than traditional motorcycle practice. Bolted to the rear of the crankshaft was a flywheel housing a twin plate dry clutch, and a shaft final drive, the shaft inside the right side of the swingarm. A universal joint connected the gearbox layshaft, with a pair of bevel gears in the rear hub. It was a robust design well suited to the police use it was intended for. More motorcycle in design was the four-speed constant mesh gearbox that bolted to the rear of the crankcase. Other areas where the V7 departed from usual motorcycle practice were the electrical and starting systems; the 12 volt electrical system incorporated a 300 watt Marelli dynamo, and starting was electric only.

The double cradle tubular steel frame was more conventional in layout, but constructed with strength rather than lightness in mind. Telescopic forks and swingarm rear suspension completed the chassis specification, and the wheels were alloy Borrani 18 inch front and rear. The 220mm drum brakes were marginal, especially given a substantial weight of 243kg. Although top speed was a claimed 170kph (105mph) with the rider fully prone, the early V7 was hardly a performance machine.

Production of the V7 was delayed due to Moto Guzzi going into receivership in February 1966. In February 1967, a new company – SEIMM (Società Esercizio Industrie Moto Meccaniche, or a company managing engineering industries) – was formed. Romolo De Stefani was installed as manager, and Donato Cattaneo as chairman in 1968. De Stefani came from Bianchi, bringing along Lino Tonti as chief engineer and Luciano Gazzola as tester. Tonti had enjoyed a long and illustrious career in the Italian motorcycle industry, previously associated with Benelli, Aermacchi, Mondial, Gilera, and Bianchi, and also strong racing connections due to involvement with Paton and Linto racing, and some street machines that bore his name. Gazzola was a leading racer in smaller capacity, Italian racing classes during the 1960s, and would prove invaluable as a development rider for the V7 and later V7 Sport.

Soon after joining Moto Guzzi, Tonti set about developing the V7. At that time the United States was the largest market for the model but Berliner, the US importer, wanted a larger capacity motorcycle. The V7 proved too slow in police acceleration tests, and Berliner needed a faster machine to secure the big police contracts. Guzzi responded by sending two tuned 750s to the US, specifically for police speed trials, and quickened development of the 750. Tonti increased the bore to 83mm, providing 757.486cc, and also adapted the V7 for speed record attempts at Monza in June 1969.

The V7 may have seemed an unlikely basis for such ventures, but Tonti managed to create two remarkably light and powerful machines: a 757cc engine for the 1000cc class, and a slightly smaller 739.35cc (83x70mm) engine for 750cc records. Compression was increased to 9.6:1, and with two 38mm Dell'Orto SS carburettors, power for both engines – 68 horsepower at 6500rpm – was similar. A 5th gear was added to the stock 4-speed gearbox. The bikes still used standard V7 Special frames, swingarm, wheels and forks, but featured a 29 litre alloy fuel tank and alloy dolphin racing-style fairing, but were remarkably light at 158kg. Top speed was around 230kph (143mph).

With chief test rider, Gazzola, out with a broken leg, four riders – Remo Venturi, Vittoria Brambilla, Guido Mandracci, and Angelo Tenconi – set three new 750cc records (100 kilometre, 1000 kilometre, and one hour). This success prompted Moto Guzzi to attempt further records a few months later in October. This time a larger team of riders went to Monza, attempting solo and sidecar classes. Silvano Bertarelli, Alberto Pagani, Franco Trabalzini, racing journalist Roberto Patrignani, Giuseppe Dal Toè, and George Auerbacher were added to the team. 19 new records were set, including the 1000cc 100 and 1000 kilometre, and hour solo records. The 100 kilometre was completed at 218.426kph (136mph), and the 1000 kilometre at 205.932kph (128mph). The hour record was set at 217.040kph (135mph). The 739cc special Guzzi also completed 12 hours at 179.553kph (111mph).

It wasn't only speed attempts that the V7 was adapted for as the bikes were also entered in occasional production races (more for testing than the expectation of race success), generally ridden by Gazzola, Jan Kampen, Raimondo Riva, and Luciano Rossi. Here, the downfall of the V7 loop frame in

Remo Venturi was one of four riders to set three 750cc world speed records at Monza in June 1969. (Courtesy Ivar de Gier)

Top right: The world record bikes were highly modified V7s. (Courtesy Ivar de Gier)

Right: Many of the records that were set were for sidecars. Here is long-time Guzzi mechanic, Ettore Casadio, fitting the solo machine with a sidecar. (Courtesy Ivar de Gier)

racing became more evident, and was the reason the V7 wasn't as popular in short circuit racing as the Laverda and Norton twins, and Triumph triple. With a single backbone tied to the rear loop, there was insufficient strength between the steering head and swingarm pivot. While this could be improved, the frame was very large and tall, and the engine too low for sufficient ground clearance.

Jan Kampen and George Kerker had already shown it was possible to achieve the aspired goals with the V7 Sport (200kph, 200kg, and 5 speeds), but rather than design new engine cases for more cornering clearance and convert the existing loop frame, Tonti decided to build a new frame. This would be used for one of Moto Guzzi's finest sporting models, the V7 Sport, and eventually the range of touring machines as well. Thus, the V7 Sport which appeared in 1971 was not only a magnificent sporting motorcycle, but also the forerunner of a long and distinguished line of performance Moto Guzzis.

The V7 eventually grew to 757cc and became the 850 GT, or Eldorado, at the same time as the V7 Sport entered production.

Micucci's 3x3 Autoveicolo da Montagna provided some design features for the V7 and eventual V7 Sport. (Courtesy Ivar de Gier)

200kph & 200kg: the V7 Sport (1971-73)

The early 1970s was an age of the emerging Superbike, and a halcyon era for the Italian motorcycle industry. While the Japanese were introducing fast and powerful, large capacity machines, their designs were about the engine rather than the chassis. British manufacturers were creating Superbikes that handled well, but were powered by obsolete motors. Only the Italians combined race-bred handling and braking with modern engine design. When it came to producing a balanced Superbike with a modern reliable engine that didn't overpower the chassis, Italian manufacturers were at the forefront. In 1971, no fewer than five Italian manufacturers were involved in the production of Superbikes: Benelli (650); Ducati (750 GT); Laverda (750 SF and SFC); MV Agusta (750 S), and Moto Guzzi (V7 Sport). Built before the onset of noise, emission regulations and cost accounting, these motorcycles epitomised the finest attributes of a golden era. Now acknowledged classics, initially, they were all produced in limited quantities, primarily for the Italian market.

In many interviews with Lino Tonti, Luciano Gazzola, and Bruno Scola, often on the upper terrace of the Hotel Grigna in Mandello, Ivar de Gier managed to trace the history of the V7 Sport, which went back to when the IMI (Instituto Mobiliare Italiano), a group of creditors chaired by Arnaldo Marcantonio, took over control of the company in 1966. (Production of the V7 was delayed due to Moto Guzzi going into receivership in February 1966.

According to Tonti: "... the decline in motorcycle sales between 1964 and 1966 created a serious financial situation for Moto Guzzi. There was no longer a market for utilitarian motorcycles and after IMI intervened it conducted some market research. This revealed a trend towards large capacity sporting and recreational machines, with an emphasis on fashionable colour schemes. After the formation of SEIMM in 1967 a decision was made to revive Moto Guzzi focusing on this market research." According to an internal memo of 1969, SEIMM leased the factory from March 1967, purchasing it outright in 1969 "... in order to make the necessary changes to ensure the survival of the company."

As previously noted, SEIMM hired Tonti and Gazzola, primarily to help fulfil the goal of building a large capacity sporting motorcycle. Tonti investigated the existing Guzzi range, reporting to the management his conclusion that: "... the V7 engine was sound and could be used as a basis for a more sporting design." He then began to develop the V7, first discarding the Dell'Orto SS1 carburettors and creating the 757 at Berliner's request in the US. As Berliner's request coincided with research into a more powerful V7, each project catalysed the other. The 750cc prototypes ran flawlessly and, as a result, existing 700s were converted into 750s. They were exported to the US as "ambassadors for the future", and the name stuck.

At the same time Tonti was considering how to build a more sporting model, and entered V7s in selected short and long distance races during 1969. The bikes proved reliable but the chassis was flawed. The front lower engine mount was too low and wide, and the nut ground prematurely. After installing a high tensile steel bolt and thinner hexagonal nut, Tonti managed to only slightly increase ground

Lino Tonti astride a prototype V7 Special with front alternator at the Monza record sessions in 1969. Even at this early stage there were plans to replace the heavy generator. (Courtesy Ivar de Gier)

clearance. Accepting that improving the chassis was something that couldn't be achieved immediately, Tonti decided to modify the engine.

The first step was to move the generator from the top to the front of the crankshaft. The Marelli 300 watt, belt-driven generator absorbed too much power, and ran too hot; sometimes the belt disintegrated at high speed, and on a few occasions even caught fire! Tonti conducted these experiments with chain drive as the engine cases required too much alteration for gears, but as the chain also absorbed too much power the eventual V7 Sport received a gear drive.

Removing the top-mounted generator meant Tonti could now mount the engine higher in the chassis. Unfortunately, this created problems with the shaft drive as the U-joints now wore excessively and contributed to a loss of power. The centre of gravity was also too high, as was the seating position.

Tonti eventually came to the conclusion that a new chassis would have to be developed in order to meet the requirements of a large capacity, luxurious sporting motorcycle. To Moto Guzzi, luxurious also meant a line of accessories (such as a plexiglas fairing), and the highest quality components. And Tonti considered a 5-speed gearbox a necessity.

By the October 1969 Monza world record sessions, Tonti already had an outline for a new motorcycle and the concept was finalised during these sessions with Managing Director, Romolo De Stefani, and FIM president, Dore Leto di Priolo. Their requirement was that the motorcycle needed to be capable of 200kph (124mph), weigh less than 200kg, and have a five-speed gearbox.

The success of the record bikes indicated that there was sufficient power to be had from the engine, and Tonti had enough experience with racing frames for Bianchi, Linto, and Paton to transform the V7 into

200KPH & 200KG: THE V7 SPORT (1971-1973)

a lithe, high performance sporting machine. The record bikes already had a five-speed gearbox, and thus the V7 Sport was born. One of the outstanding sporting motorcycles of the era, it displayed Tonti's genius at its best. Others were also developing the V7, and with his V7 Kampen Express, Dutchman Jan Kampen proved it could become an acceptable sports machine.

V7 Sport prototypes

With De Stefani's blessing Tonti began work on the V7 Sport immediately after the Monza speed runs. Tonti's intention was to implement production after the traditional holiday break in August 1970, having the machine on the market in 1971 to celebrate Moto Guzzi's 50th anniversary. Unfortunately, this didn't eventuate as the factory at Mandello was beset by strikes. Moto Guzzi wasn't the only company affected by industrial problems, which continued throughout northern Italy at this time and over the next few years.

Tonti began by designing a frame around the final version of the front-mounted generator engine created in the lead-up to the speed runs. To avoid interruptions caused by rolling strikes, Tonti – with the help of two former Aermacchi colleagues, Francesco Botta (assisting in the design) and Alcide Biotti (helping with fabrication) – built two prototype V7 Sport frames. Tonti then built a complete bike in his own workshop, and with Botta and Biotti, a second bike at Moto Guzzi. Although the goal was to build a road bike, as a firm believer in the premise that 'racing improves the breed', Tonti designed the frame primarily for racing with predominantly straight tubes as was accepted practice. (This frame design, known now as the 'Tonti' frame, features on all the Moto Guzzi V-twins included in this book.) The frame tubes tied outboard of the swingarm pivot for greater rigidity, and to reduce deflection under cornering load. With the generator gone there was more space between the cylinders, allowing a much lower frame backbone. To facilitate engine access the lower frame rails were removable. Further weight saving included a smaller Bosch starter motor, lighter forks, and slimmer stainless steel mudguards. Prior to completion of the new engine design, Tonti mounted one of the record-breaking, October 1969 engines in the new frame and took it to Monza. Because of the improved brakes and handling, Gazzola lapped six seconds faster than he had on the earlier machine.

The first prototype was ready by early 1970, and tested by Gazzola and Tonti on the streets and mountains around Lake Como. During one of these tests Tonti crashed the machine, breaking his leg. Undeterred, he had the leg set with the knee bent far enough so that he could still ride, and incorporated a special mount to carry his crutches. The first prototypes were built as racing machines, not street bikes as is often believed. Long and low, they featured the longer tank that was used on later racing bikes, an empty triangle where

Mike Hailwood astride an early prototype V7 Sport at Monza in 1971. (Courtesy Ivar de Gier)

the later toolboxes would be, clip-on handlebars, Ceriani front fork, and a racing open exhaust system. On seeing the prototype, Ivar de Gier said: "That thing was low. I always had the impression it was lower then the later ones, but looks can be deceiving and I never had it confirmed. They were built purely for track testing mainly at Monza, and were raced in non-production events during 1971 and 1972, with a full fairing and different engine." Tonti told Ivar "... by the middle of 1970, all the production drawings were ready to manufacture the V7 Sport." All Tonti had to do now was persuade the management to proceed with production ...

There was no doubt that Tonti had created a masterpiece, but when Alberici, the production manager, looked at the prototype he noted there had been at least 151 changes compared to the V7 (Alberici was mistaken to think this as the V7 Sport was a completely new machine). He also wasn't convinced of the merits of implementing the production of an expensive sporting motorcycle, even if Tonti had met the required criteria of 200kph, 200kg and five speeds. A disagreement followed, with Tonti handing management his letter of resignation. A shocked and surprised management investigated what had occurred between Tonti and Alberici, and whether the new machine fulfilled its design goal.

Alberici and Tonti were interviewed, as were all others involved in the development. As Guzzi wanted to be sure that the V7 Sport would succeed in the market, outside consultants were engaged to examine all the data. Management learnt of the Monza "six second story" and were soon aware that this was a great sports bike with some excellent features. But the "six second story" was not enough to persuade it to go ahead. After a long investigation it wasn't until the autumn of 1970 that a final decision was made and the V7 Sport received the go-ahead. Tonti was happy but also frustrated, as he wanted the bike in production during 1971. Time was running out to achieve that, and although Tonti began developing the prototype for production in September 1970, there were still many problems to overcome. The V7 Sport was essentially all-new, and it wasn't possible to prepare the tools and dies. There was also no room on the production line, and the company was still stricken by long and regular strikes. As 1971 was an important year for Guzzi, a decision was made to build a first batch in the racing department. These were pre-production Telaio Rossi, with many handmade components, such as the fuel tank. All of them were slightly different, and they had modified Dingo electrical components (handlebar switches). These early bikes were built for racing and testing by motorcycle journalists.

Hailwood initially rode the V7 Sport dressed for a magazine car test he was undertaking at the time. (Courtesy Ivar de Gier)

Ducati had generated considerable publicity for the impending 750 by displaying prototypes to the press more than a year prior to regular production, and Moto Guzzi followed suit. By the time the V7 Sport was widely available it was well publicised.

Tonti unveiled his creation in June 1971 at the Monza 500 kilometre race for 750cc production machines. (This was a promising debut, and is covered in Chapter 7.) To ensure the bike was competitive, Mike Hailwood tested it at Monza prior to the race, afterwards proclaiming the V7 Sport the best handling street bike he had ridden. Although more involved in racing Formula 2 cars, Hailwood was to test a Telaio Rosso on several occasions. Press versions were despatched to magazines in Italy and Germany in September, and two examples put on display at the Milan Show in November 1971: one had a red frame and small plexiglas fairing, and the other a black-painted frame. Some of the early test and show bikes also included more rounded and louder Lafranconi mufflers, instead of the usual Silentium versions.

An example of the lengths Moto Guzzi went to to source the highest quality components was evident in the plexiglas fairing. Requiring a screen that didn't distort the rider's view, Guzzi approached many companies, Gazzola eventually finding one in a small town near Voghera. Although this company claimed it could produce such a screen, it took much experimentation to achieve the required result.

Telaio Rosso

Early examples of the V7 Sport can be considered pre-production models, hand built examples before

Hailwood about to ride one of the two prototype V7 Sports prepared for the 1971 Monza 500km race. (Courtesy Ivar de Gier)

regular production was implemented. The FIM required at least 100 bikes to be manufactured to homologate the V7 Sport for production racing, and official factory data indicates 104 were built in 1971. This first production series continued briefly into 1972 and has become known as the Telaio Rosso (Red Frame) series because most were distinguished by a red-painted frame. IMI's market research of 1967 had shown fashionable colour schemes to be important to the consumer, and a Milan design institute was consulted for advice. This resulted in the red and white combination implemented on the V7, and later Stornello and Falcone Civile. For the V7 Sport the design institute recommended an extravagant green and red, which received Moto Guzzi's approval. These colours were not deliberately chosen to create an association with Guzzi's racing past, as is commonly believed, however, as the lime green for the tank and tool boxes was nothing like the zinc-chromate green of the 1950s dustbin racers, and those bikes never

Two V7 Sports were displayed at the 1971 Milan Show; one with the small fairing and the other a black frame. (Courtesy Ivar de Gier)

raced with a red frame. Another Tonti project of the same era, the prototype Ghezz, also received a green and red colour scheme. This green was similar to the racing green, indicating Guzzi was experimenting with colours. The first examples of the Telaio Rosso were painted a very light green, though not as yellow as it appears in period brochures, which are very unreliable colour guides.

Although the Telaio Rosso can be considered pre-production, all examples carried official engine and frame numbers. Engine numbers began at VK 30000 and frame numbers at VK 11111. The frame numbers were stamped on the steering head and, although some publications have claimed there were some V7 Sports with a C (Corsa) or even a VKC prefix, Lino Tonti told Ivar de Gier that all production V7 Sports had a VK prefix (factory racing versions originally did not have a VK number). All frames with a VK prefix carried a stamped homologation number: DGM 9104 OM.

The engine numbers were stamped on the left crankcase. According to the factory parts catalogue, the Telaio Rosso series consisted of 150 machines, indicating they finished at frame VK 11261 and engine VK 30151. The first edition of the owners' and workshop manuals supports this, showing engine number VK 30156 as a production example with a black-painted frame. There was some inconsistency in production numbers as Telaio Rossi continued to be produced for racing when necessary, and also prior to completion of the production line early in 1972. Umberto Todero told leading Moto Guzzi historian Ivar de Gier that a total of 204 Telaio Rossi were produced, while Tonti, Gazzola and Bruno Scola said only 150 were built. Gazzola passionately stated to de Gier that only 150 were built. Ivar doubts

The factory released a series of publicity photos of the Telaio Rosso in 1971. This one is signed by Luciano Gazzola. (Courtesy Ivar de Gier)

Todero's claim and believes that only 150 Telaio Rosso had VK numbers, and the few extra bikes were racing versions that were never numbered. Gazzola and Tonti both indicated that 5 to 10 frames were kept as spares for racing.

After the regular black frame series V7 Sport went into production, Guzzi no longer supplied the chrome molybdenum frame as a spare part, instead keeping it as a replacement in the event of crashes. The 850 sport prototypes, like the 'Premio Varrone' bikes (see Chapter 4), used the Telaio Rosso frame. Occasionally, a special bike was constructed after the 150 production run for a specific customer, using a Telaio Rosso frame with production engine and chassis components. It is documented that Formula One car racing world champion, Emerson Fittipaldi, received one of these machines, with a larger racing Fontana front brake, in September 1972. Other Formula One car drivers who tested the Telaio Rosso included Jacky Ickx. Although much has been made of the special nature of the Telaio Rossi, Ivar believes there were fewer differences between the Telaio Rosso and the regular production series than is commonly believed. It was the extra care in assembly and construction that set the Telaio Rosso apart from later examples. Complicating the documentation is that most Telaio Rosso differed slightly from each other as they were hand built models that used what was available at the time of manufacture.

Engine and transmission

On the Telaio Rosso the engine castings were sand-cast. (The rough, sand-cast finish was quite different to later production castings and is the easiest way to distinguish this model.) The sump and crankcases included more external ribbing than the V7, and displacement was reduced slightly, to 748cc, to enable the V7 Sport to compete in 750cc production racing. In addition to a new timing case for the front-mounted alternator, vents were incorporated from the valve covers to the breather box.

The four-ring pistons measured 82.5mm, and compression ratio increased to 9.8:1. As on the V7, the cylinders were chrome-plated. The cylinder head with 72mm chamber (a depth of 26mm), and valve sizes of 41 and 36mm was the same as that used on the V7 Special. The two valves were also inclined at the same 70 degree angle, which was slightly more up-to-date than that of some contemporary Italian motorcycles (such as the Ducati and MV Agusta 750). Contrary to folklore, the cylinder heads were stamped with part numbers (although some of the later production series weren't). The valves had 8mm stems, the inlet valve was 107mm long and the exhaust valve 105mm. Aluminium valve collars and double valve springs were employed: a 52.5mm outer and 45mm inner.

The V7 Sport received a new camshaft with more valve lift and increased duration compared to the V7 Special. The inlet valve now opened 40 degrees before top dead centre, closing 70 degrees after bottom dead centre, and the exhaust valve opened 63 degrees before top dead centre and closed 29 degrees after bottom dead centre. Valve lift for both valves was 6.9mm. Camshaft drive was by a set of steel helical gears from the front of the crankshaft, the three gears including a crankshaft 31 tooth, camshaft 52 tooth, and 26 tooth oil pump gear. This camshaft was used on all V7 Sports and the 750S until 1974.

Carburettor sizes increased slightly from 29mm to 30mm, the square-slide Dell'Orto VHB 30 carburettors fitted with accelerator pumps. The accelerator pump was a rudimentary affair, featuring a spring-loaded plunger that was depressed by the metering needle when the throttle was closed. Typical of Italian motorcycles of this period, there were no air cleaners, although the carburettors were fed via a rubber airbox to reduce intake noise and provide a rudimentary air filtration system. Apparently, Lino Tonti didn't incorporate a filter in the airbox because the intake air had to turn so many corners that the heavier dirt particles couldn't get through the intake manifolds. With 70 horsepower at 7000rpm produced at the crankshaft (52 horsepower at 6300rpm at the rear wheel), the V7 Sport was one of the most powerful motorcycles available in 1971.

To cope with this increase in power the lower end was considerably strengthened. The forged, one-piece steel crankshaft and two-piece con-rods were polished, with special con-rod bolts and nuts. The main and big-end bearings were AL-TIN alloy. The big-end journals measured 44mm, and the big-end eye 47mm, with a 22mm gudgeon pin. The gudgeons were relatively light, with an internal bore of 15mm. Con-rod length was 140mm eye-to-eye, providing a near-perfect stroke to rod length ratio of 2:1, and the crankshaft journals measured 38 and 54mm at the flywheel. The crankshaft was supported by large aluminium carriers bolted into the crankcase. The flywheel was much lighter than on the V7 and featured different ignition timing marks, increasing ignition advance to a total of 39 degrees. Lubrication was by a high pressure oil pump driven from the crankshaft, providing oil pressure of 3.8-4.2kg/m^2 (54-60lb/in^2). This oil pump was so efficient and reliable that it featured on all sporting Guzzis included in this book. As on the V7, there was no oil filter on the V7 Sport, although bosses were cast for its later inclusion. Oil filtration was by a wire gauze in the bottom of the crankcase.

Carburation on the V7 Sport was via square-slide Dell'Orto VHB 30 carburettors. There was no air filter. The fuel petcock on the left was solenoid operated. (Courtesy Two Wheels)

A twin-plate, flywheel-driven dry clutch fed the power to the five-speed transmission via the 16/22 (1.375:1) primary drive of the V7 and V7 Special. The clutch unit was retained by the starter motor ring gear and included 8 springs inside the flywheel housing. Inside the smooth, sand-cast transmission case was a new five-speed gearbox, with a unique set of ratios for the Telaio Rosso. Built by specialist gear company, Tenagli, of Pontedera in Tuscany, not only were the ratios unique, but most of the internal components were specific to the Telaio Rosso; this included the shaft, sleeves bushes and shifting forks. Because of the five-speed gearbox, the transmission case was exclusive to the Telaio Rosso and not shared with the V7. The design of the five-speed gearbox echoed that of the record bikes. The V7 three-shaft design was retained but with a fifth gear added to the mainshaft and layshaft. As on the record bikes, fifth gear was added on and the gear width was less than the other gears. Needle bearings replaced the bushings on the gears and the Tenagli gearbox was also used on the production Telaio Rosso (and would prove one of the weakest components). It was not particularly durable, with fifth gear especially troublesome and prone to failure. But due to the care of assembly

Right side view of the Telaio Rosso. The smooth cast transmission case is evident. (Courtesy Ivar de Gier)

200KPH & 200KG: THE V7 SPORT (1971-1973)

Rear three-quarter view shows the earlier dimpled rear drive unit and sharply cut off Silentium mufflers. (Courtesy Ivar de Gier)

and close manufacturing tolerances, the Tenagli gearbox shifted impeccably, considerably better than the later production transmission. Only a few replacement components were ever available for the Tenagli gearbox and most units were replaced by later gearboxes. The gearshift was on the right, the traditional Italian one-up and four-down shift facilitated by a beautifully crafted, Heim joint linkage. The polished one-piece cast rear drive unit was the same as on the V7, and included six external dimples, and a single drain plug at the rear. The rear drive gears were blue-printed and carefully assembled, and a taller ratio (8/35) compensated for the smaller section rear tyre.

The V7 Sport was also fitted with a new ignition system, including a Marelli S311A distributor with twin points, and twin Marelli BM200C coils (replacing the V7's single point distributor and coil). The exhaust system included extremely quiet Silentium mufflers with 'shark-fin'-style ends, although the Lafranconi muffler (also built in Mandello) of some early pre-production and show examples was also specified as an option. The original Silentium mufflers were sharply cut-off, unlike modern reproduction replacement mufflers.

The single wall exhaust header pipes were threaded into the cylinder head and connected by two crossover balance tubes underneath the transmission. The single wall exhaust headers went noticeably blue almost immediately. Unique to the V7 Sport (and later 750 S and S3), were smaller diameter front and rear exhaust clamps than the crossover and muffler clamps.

Frame
The frames were constructed of thin wall chrome molybdenum (1.5-2mm thickness), and generally painted red (with a black centre stand). In addition to the frame number the Telaio Rosso frame was also homologated by the Italian Ministero dei Transporti e dell'Aviazione Civile, carrying homologation number DGM 9104 OM stamped on the steering head, near the frame number. As the Telaio Rosso frame was not mass produced, there were many variations from later examples: the lower frame tube was formed and not flat, and the rear section had a different rear seat pivot point as there were different lugs. Swingarm length was 390mm.

Suspension
The 35mm front forks with polished alloy fork legs were hand built, and manufactured by Moto Guzzi. The design included internal springs and sealed internal dampers. Although originally innovative, the cartridge-type forks were not particularly sophisticated and effective. The dampers were a Savena-type, 22x8mm, produced by Lims. To reduce frontal area the fork legs were closer together – 180mm apart – than on the V7, and had a stroke of 125mm. Fork springs were 421mm long. For a sports motorcycle the front fork had quite soft springing, the assembled spring providing a load of 11.3kg when compressed (BY?) 16mm. An adjustable Lims hydraulic steering damper was controlled by a black plastic knob on the top triple clamp.

The rear suspension was the best Tonti could find: 320mm Dutch Koni 76F 1267 shock absorbers with chrome-plated springs. Compared to most other shock absorbers of the early 1970s, the Konis were considerable stronger, with longer springs (277mm free length), and 36mm shock bodies. The shock absorber travel was a generous 85mm.

Wheels and brakes
To provide quick steering the V7 Sport rode on narrow, 18 inch wheels. Borrani alloy rims were traditional on sporting Italian motorcycles, but Tonti specified the stronger Cross type laced with 40 straight pull stainless steel spokes. The front was a Borrani WM2/18 Record RM01 4645 Cross (1.85x18 inch), and the rear a Borrani WM3/18 Record RM01 4666 Cross (2.15x18 inch). The four-leading shoe front brake (220x25x25mm) looked impressive but, whilst performance was on a par with most other drum brakes of the day, it was ineffective compared to the next generation of disc brakes. At the rear

was a full width, 200x25mm, double leading shoe, operated by a cable on the left. Tyres were the latest generation Michelin; a ribbed 3.25 L25 on the front and 3.50 S41 on the rear, reputedly specially developed by Michelin for the V7 Sport. Some bikes were fitted with a 3.25x18 inch S41 tyre on the front.

Bodywork and fittings

When it came to detail design, in 1971 the V7 Sport was unequalled. Unlike comparable limited edition, Italian production racing motorcycles that used mostly fibreglass body components, the V7 Sport was fitted with a steel fuel tank and lockable steel tool boxes. The front and rear mudguards were also stainless steel.

On the Telaio Rosso, fuel tank and seat size and shape were not consistent. The seats were produced by Gaman in Milan on a steel base, and early and later examples featured slightly smaller tanks and a different seat. Most Telaio Rossi had a slightly larger fuel tank (22.5 litre), and lugs which were different to those of later production versions. The only convenience feature not present was a locking fuel filler cap. The cap hinged forward, opening away from the rider, and was the ubiquitous chrome-plated type that appeared on nearly all Italian motorcycles of this period (including Ducati and Laverda). These early caps featured a 60mm seal. The fuel taps were Brev Orlandi R91/1, with a Sirai 2.5 watt electromagnetic tap on the left. Specific to the green Telaio Rosso fuel tank were decals with a black strip and red and white highlighting; 'MOTO GUZZI' in white, and a gold eagle. Some of the first prototypes featured decals without the eagle.

The spot welded, stainless steel rear fender was split, pivoting so the seat could fold upward. While this feature continued on the production V7 Sport, the pivot point was different. Also unique were the adjustable swan-neck, clip-on handlebars, particularly elegant on the Telaio Rosso because they were machine forged and hand bent. The handlebars could be positioned higher or lower on the fork tubes as the headlight was supported by a special crinkle black-painted curved alloy casting. Engine protection bars were optional, but there was no side stand on the Telaio Rosso. Attention to detail and symmetry extended to the footpegs and controls. The gearshift and brake pedals were mirror images of each other, and the footpegs sat on forged steel brackets that were so beautifully finished they looked as if they were made of aluminium. The footpeg position was semi-sporting, placing the rider's feet 40mm below the swingarm pivot and 75mm in front. The handgrip and footpeg rubbers were in matching patterns. Some of the plastic inserts were also white, unlike later bikes,

The front end of the V7 Sport; four-leading shoe drum brake, Borrani Cross light alloy wheel, and a 35mm fork with sealed dampers. (Courtesy Two Wheels)

which featured black inserts. The throttle was aluminium Magura, and many of the fasteners were chrome-plated.

Electrical system and instrumentation

The quality of the electrical system was also a departure from traditional Italian motorcycle practice that favoured minimal electrics and kick-starting. Powered by a Bosch V114-A13 180 watt alternator, and 12 volt 32 Ah battery, only an electric start was specified. To save weight this was a small Bosch DG (L) 12V 0.4 PS, centrifugally-engaged type, mostly produced in Spain. Only 0.4 horsepower, it lacked a solenoid, but included an external relay mounted on a bracket to the transmission. This starting system could result in damage to the flywheel's ring gear, and was one of the least reliable features of the V7 Sport.

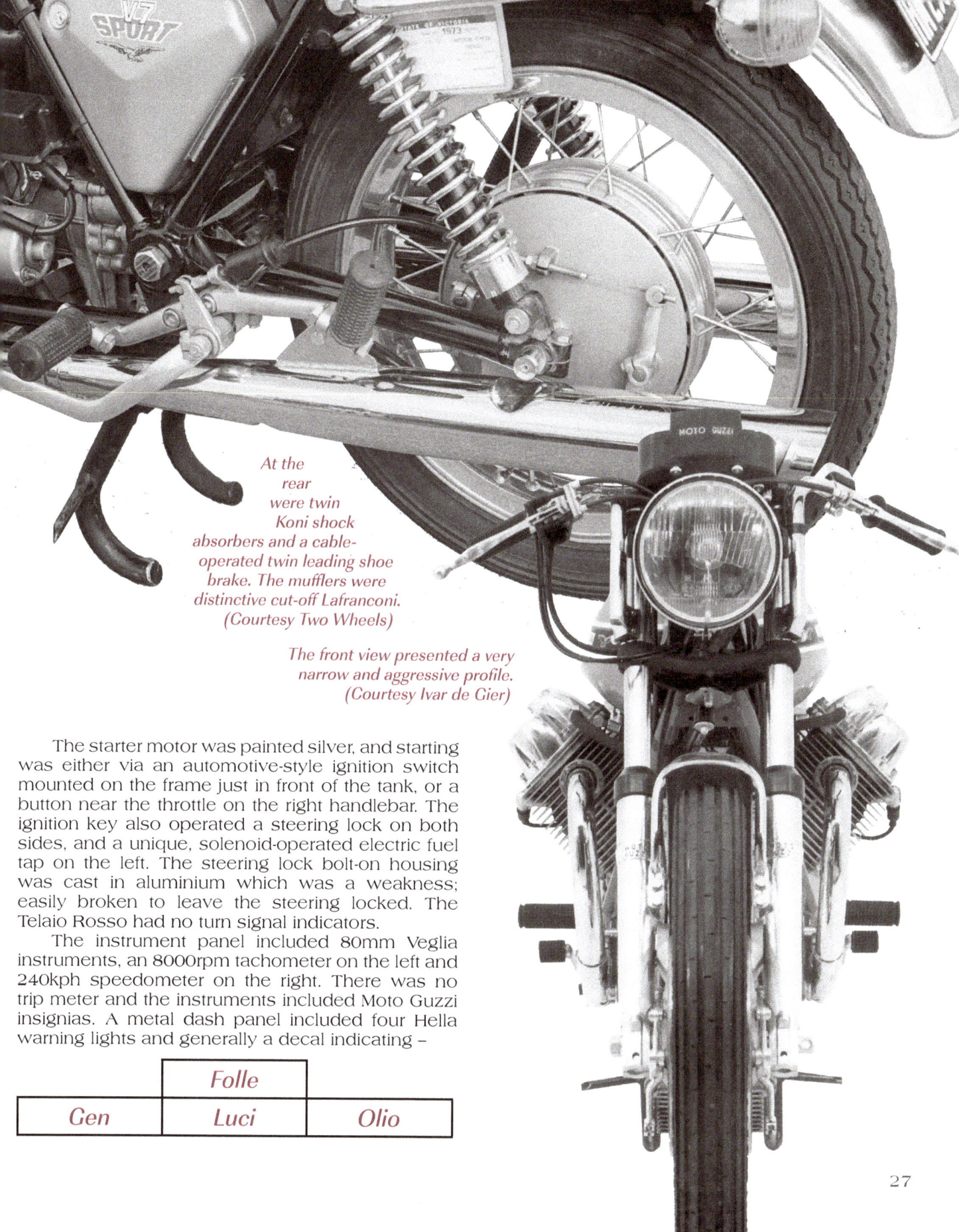

At the rear were twin Koni shock absorbers and a cable-operated twin leading shoe brake. The mufflers were distinctive cut-off Lafranconi. (Courtesy Two Wheels)

The front view presented a very narrow and aggressive profile. (Courtesy Ivar de Gier)

The starter motor was painted silver, and starting was either via an automotive-style ignition switch mounted on the frame just in front of the tank, or a button near the throttle on the right handlebar. The ignition key also operated a steering lock on both sides, and a unique, solenoid-operated electric fuel tap on the left. The steering lock bolt-on housing was cast in aluminium which was a weakness; easily broken to leave the steering locked. The Telaio Rosso had no turn signal indicators.

The instrument panel included 80mm Veglia instruments, an 8000rpm tachometer on the left and 240kph speedometer on the right. There was no trip meter and the instruments included Moto Guzzi insignias. A metal dash panel included four Hella warning lights and generally a decal indicating –

	Folle	
Gen	Luci	Olio

The light and horn handlebar switch was the usual, rectangular CEV as fitted to other Italian motorcycles, as, too, were the twin Voxbell Belli horns mounted on the front frame downtubes. The Telaio Rossi had a small light under the folding seat,

The V7 Sport instrument panel was amongst the most comprehensive of any motorcycle in 1971. Starting was either by the ignition key or a button on the right near the throttle. (Courtesy Two Wheels)

while CEV (an electrical company) provided the 170mm mod 4507 headlight, and small round mod 9335 taillight.

Certainly Tonti achieved his objective of creating a five-speed sporting motorcycle that weighed around 200kg and was capable of 200kph; the eventual claimed figures were 206kg (453 pounds), and 206kph (129mph). Most Telaio Rossi were sold in Italy, with only a few examples going to other countries. In the UK, Rivetts of Leytonstone was the official distributor, and at £1350 it was the most expensive motorcycle available in Britain. Rivetts provided an example for testing to various magazines, including *Motor Cycle News*, *Motorcycle Mechanics* and *Motorcycle Sport*.

Very few Telaio Rossi were sent to the US. According to factory records, the only official Telaio Rosso was sent to George Kerker. Berliner also received one – painted red, with silver tank decals and a silver frame – but this does not appear in factory records as a Telaio Rosso. This was tested by *Cycle* magazine in its July 1972 issue. Known as the Mike Berliner Special, later, it was sent back to Italy, returning black with a black frame. Ivar de Gier discussed the history of this machine with Gazzola and Tonti, and it appears many Telaio

Underneath the lifting seat was a small courtesy light. (Courtesy Two Wheels)

V7 Sport Telaio Rosso distinguishing features (from frame number VK 11111-VK 11261; engine number VK 30001-VK 30151)

Engine
Right cylinder head identified by part number 14022100
Left cylinder head identified by part number 14022200
Valve rocker covers polished with different part numbers 14023500 right and 14023600 left
Polished and lightened valve rockers
Polished crankshaft
Polished con-rods with different con-rod bolts and nuts part number 12062280/12062380
Engine castings sand-cast
Transmission case cast smooth, without ribs and part number 14208280
Transmission shaft bearings different (25x52x12mm and 14x47x14 mm)
Most transmission components unique to the Telaio Rosso
Straight clutch arm
Primary drive ratio 16/22 (1.375:1)
First gear: 15/27 (1.8:1)
Second gear: 19/24 (1.263:1)
Third gear: 22/21 (0.954:1)
Fourth gear: 24/19 (0.791:1)
Fifth gear: 25/17 (0.680:1)
Final drive: 8/35 (4.375:1) (optional 9/37 or a 'Sport' 8/37)

Frame
Frame constructed of chrome molybdenum (NiCrMo) tubing 1.5-2mm
The lower frame tube was formed, with a different rear seat pivot point, and different lugs.
Machine forged adjustable handlebars
Different speedometer and tachometer pods and tachometer drive
Several series of fuel tanks, most larger than later examples with different lugs
Different seat to match larger fuel tank
Rear mudguard spot welded with different pivot points for folding
Some plastic inserts in foot controls were white
Many chrome-plated fasteners

Rosso parts were replaced with regular production components that were more readily available at the time. Gazzola also believed the frame was replaced by the production prototype steel frame, originally red, then painted black. This frame differed to the Telaio Rosso and also the production frame. Most of Berliner's requests were to change the colours. Tonti and Gazzola confirmed with Ivar that the mechanics were told to "... replace and keep the parts that were valuable", which is probably why the MB special doesn't appear as a Telaio Rosso in the factory records.

Irrespective of the exact number of Telaio Rossi produced, it remains a limited production, hand built machine, the most sought-after of the V7 Sport model, commanding premium prices compared to later production examples. Producing special first editions wasn't unique to Moto Guzzi, and both Ducati and Laverda also indulged in this practice in the early 1970s with their 750 Super Sport and SFC respectively. Generally, and with Ducati in particular, first editions are more desirable because they are less compromised in terms of quality and equipment. During the production life of the V7 Sport (and the comparable Ducati 750), cost-cutting became evident.

Determining authenticity can be an issue with a Telaio Rosso, as more red-frame V7 Sports are in circulation than were produced, although not all of these claim to be genuine; many owners and restorers simply like the distinctive colour scheme. And as the last examples of the Telaio Rosso were built just as regular production was about to start, some of the final examples were closer in specification to the production black-frame version than earlier versions. These final Telaio Rosso were not totally hand built, and had fewer polished parts, later production handlebars, and the production front fork.

The Telaio Rosso is now considered the archetypal sporting Moto Guzzi. (Courtesy Ivar de Gier)

Production V7 Sport 1972 (first series from frame number VK 11262-VK 13204 approx)

For 1972 regular production of the V7 Sport was implemented. Although the general layout and specification was as for the Telaio Rosso, there were a number of updates. As V7 Sport series production coincided with the release of the 850 GT and Eldorado for the USA market; there was also a US-specific version. Although still not mass produced, V7 Sport production increased significantly with 2152 examples built in 1972 (including some Telaio Rosso), which would place 1972 V7 Sports through until approximately frame number VK 13253 (althoughit was usual for more frames to be built than complete motorcycles). The parts list indicates frame number VK 13205 as the start of the next series, so it can be assumed that there was some overlap in exact specification between 1972 and 1973. This is evident in my own unrestored and near-original production example VK 13209, which has some earlier features, such as the handlebars. Engine numbers for the production series continued from those of the Telaio Rosso, from VK 30151, but the engines were no longer race department assembled. As engines were assembled prior to installation in a chassis, engine and frame number correlation is inconsistent throughout the production series. Engine numbers for this frame series are known to go well beyond the expected VK 32093 that would correspond with the frame number VK 13204. Likewise, many engines with earlier numbers appeared in later frames. Because of this anomaly –

200kph & 200kg: the V7 Sport (1971-1973)

and despite US examples using engine numbers for identification – it is easier to categorise the V7 Sport by frame number.

Engine and transmission

On the production V7 Sport the crankcase and transmission castings were die-cast, the transmission casing incorporating external webbing like the crankcase. The cylinder heads and rocker covers were new, and the crankshaft and con-rods no longer polished. The con-rods also had new bolts and nuts. There were a few small changes to the ignition and carburettor jetting but, as engine specification was largely unchanged, power remained the same. From frame number VK 12700 there was revised carburettor jetting and new inlet manifolds. The aluminium pushrods were also modified slightly for the production engine with a larger steel upper. Claimed power was slightly down at 70 horsepower/7000rpm.

Most updates affected the transmission. As the earlier Tengali transmission was prone to failure – particularly 5th gear – inside the new transmission case was an updated gearbox. To increase the speed of the transmission gears, facilitating shifting, the primary drive was increased slightly to 17/21 (1.235:1) with other ratios lowered to compensate: 1st gear became 14/28; 2nd 18/25; 3rd 21/22; 4th 23/20, and 5th 24/18. Other transmission developments included larger transmission shaft bearings.

This transmission was shared with the new 850 GT and Eldorado, but was also problematic as the locking ring holding 5th gear on the mainshaft could sometimes break. 850 GTs were recalled early in 1972, presumably affecting a few early production V7 Sports. A spring and plunger was inserted to lock the inner race in place, and flanged to retain the gear. The updated transmission case was stamped with '3' near the speedometer drive. There was also a new rear drive case, now without dimples, and including a removable, six-bolt, finned sump. Oil capacity increased to 360cc from around 180cc for the earlier rear drive unit.

Chassis

While frame numbers continued the Telaio Rosso sequence from VK 11262, the frame was series-produced in mild Aq 45 steel tubing and not hand welded in chrome molybdenum. Dimensions remained unchanged, with the same formed, lower frame tubes, although the steel tubing was thicker (2.5-3mm). The new frame was undoubtedly heavier but Moto Guzzi made no revisions to the claimed dry weight of the V7 Sport. Originally, it was also going to be painted red, but this was changed to black prior to production. While the suspension was similar to the Telaio Rosso, there were new fork legs and tubes. The tubes were slightly narrower at 34.725mm. Towards the end of this series, from frame number VK 13189 there were new fork tubes,

For 1972 the V7 Sport entered production with a black-painted, mild steel frame. Another Gazzola-signed picture. (Courtesy Ivar de Gier)

With the production series of the V7 Sport came a ribbed transmission case and new, rear final drive housing. (Courtesy Two Wheels)

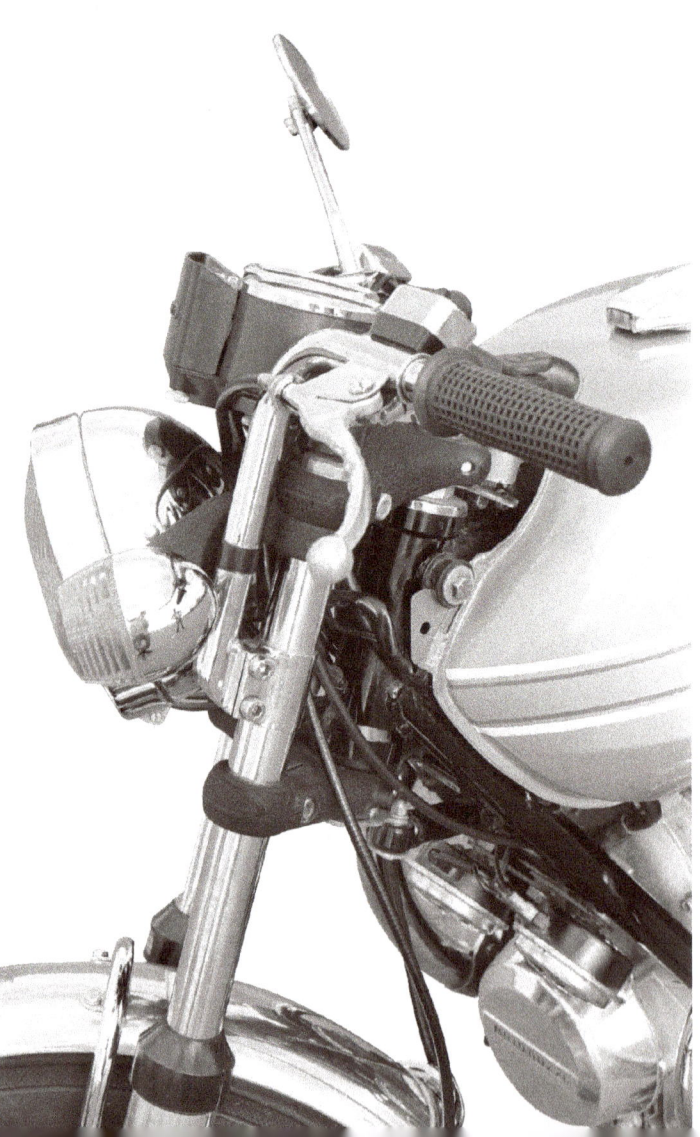

interchangeable with the earlier type and 544mm long.

The fuel tank was slightly smaller (19 litres), and the decals were changed to coincide with regular production. These fuel tanks were usually supplied by LAILA SpA of Ozzano Emilia, a company that specialized in stamped steel components. Although some early production bikes continued with the Telaio Rosso tank decals, most decals were now white lettering with red and white stripes. Colours were also generally green for the fuel tank and tool boxes, although some were red. At some stage during this series the steel fuel tank gained an additional mounting hole at the front. Other updates included a riveted (instead of spot welded) rear mudguard, and standardised tank and seat mounting points.

While the wiring system provided for Aprilia turn signals, many 1972 European examples didn't have turn signals. Some examples were also fitted with rounder-bodied CEV indicators. The underseat courtesy light remained, but there were new speedometer and tachometer pods, and a new tachometer drive. The clip-on handlebars were similar in design to the Telaio Rosso, with 8x30mm chrome bolts screwing into internal threads, but made from stamped rather than forged steel. As on the Telaio Rosso, many of the fasteners on this series of V7 Sport were chrome-plated, including

Although the adjustable handlebars looked similar to those on the Telaio Rosso, for 1972 they were stamped instead of forged steel. (Courtesy Two Wheels)

the fuel tank mounting screws, transmission drain plug, lower frame Allen bolts, rear seat securing screws, shock absorber bolts, washers and nuts, and instrument panel screws. The front and rear axles, nuts and washers were also chrome-plated. Optional equipment included large engine protection bars and a side stand (with a single spring).

Performance did not change, and the V7 Sport remained one of the fastest motorcycles available in 1972. In a Superbike comparison test in September 1972, the Italian magazine, *Motociclismo*, squeezed a top speed of 201.117kph (125mph) from a production black-frame V7 Sport; faster than any of the other 750s, including the Honda CB750 and Kawasaki H2 750. At Monza the V7 Sport lapped significantly faster than any of the other bikes in the test, which included the Ducati 750 GT and Laverda 750 SF. Weighing 212.5kg, the standing start 400 metre time was 13.44 seconds at 148.76kph (92mph).

US V7 Sport 1972 and 1973

In 1972 Moto Guzzi's US distributor was the Premier Motor Corporation, part of the Berliner group. As with the Ducatis it distributed, Berliner – or the factory – placed a plate over the stamped frame number. (This identification plate was available as an official spare

Whilst not as exotic as the Telaio Rosso, the production V7 Sport was still a handsome and imposing machine. (Courtesy Two Wheels)

Still no starter solenoid, but the early production V7 Sport did retain some chrome-plated nuts and the ball joint gearshift linkage. (Courtesy Two Wheels)

part, as were the rivets.) Because of this riveted plate the VIN (Vehicle Identification Number) for US V7 Sports was always the engine number. As the factory-stamped frame number was evident underneath the plate, it is incorrect to say that US examples had frame numbers in the VK 30000 series.

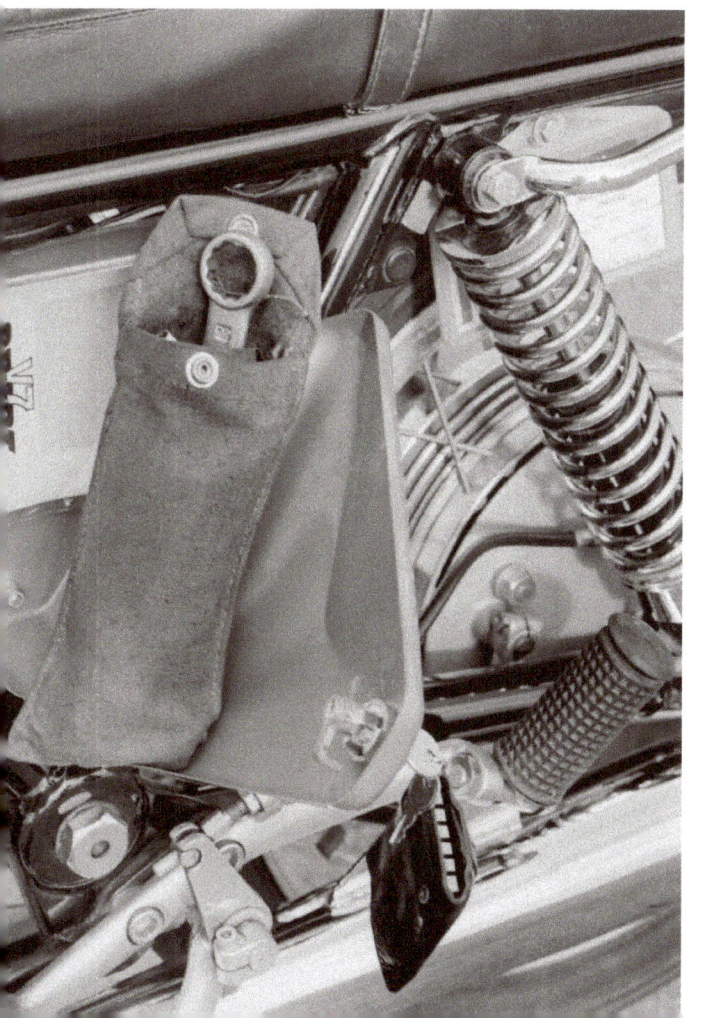

A comprehensive tool kit was contained inside the locking steel toolbox. (Courtesy Two Wheels)

The V7 Sport also had exceptional sporting performance for the day. (Courtesy Two Wheels)

V7 Sport distinguishing features 1972 (from frame number VK 11262-VK 13204; engine number VK 30151-VK 32800 approx)

Engine and transmission
New cylinder heads with stamped part number
Right cylinder head identified by part number 13022160
Left cylinder head identified by part number 13022260
Valve rocker covers not polished and with new part numbers 14023502 right and 14023602 left
Different con-rod bolts and nuts
Carburettor jetting changed 142 main jet, V9 needle (from VK 12700)
Reduced static engine advance to 13 degrees and smaller contact breaker gap
Engine castings die-cast
Transmission case-cast with strengthening external ribs
New rear transmission cover
New transmission shaft bearings (25x52x20mm RIV 3205 secondary shaft); (17x47x14mm RIV N303 primary shaft)
Primary gear ratio; 17/21 (1.235:1)
First gear: 14/18 (2:1)
Second gear: 18/25 (1.388:1)
Third gear: 21/22 (1.047:1)
Fourth gear: 23/20 (0.869:1)
Fifth gear: 24/18 (0.750:1)
New, larger capacity final drive casting, with inbuilt sump

Chassis
Frame constructed of thicker (2.5-3mm) Aq 45J mild steel and painted black (or silver on some US versions)
Fuel tank was smaller (21 litres) and gained an additional front mounting hole
Rear mudguard riveted instead of spot welded with revised pivot points
Stamped clip-on handlebars
Plastic inserts in foot controls black
New fork legs and smaller diameter 34.7mm fork tubes
New speedometer and tachometer holders
New tachometer drive
Turn signal indicator wiring standard and Aprilia or CEV turn signals available
Still many fasteners chrome-plated

Like the European versions, US V7 Sports continued with frame numbers from VK 11261. All US models featured a CEV model 4508/C sealed beam

200KPH & 200KG: THE V7 SPORT (1971-1973)

headlight, larger CEV 9359.13 taillight, and front reflectors behind the fork legs. Unlike European models that featured Aprilia turn signal indicators, US versions had British Lucas (model 874 n 56147A). A CEV switch on the right handlebar operated the turn signals. The lettering decal on the instrument panel was in English, while the Veglia speedometer read to 160mph, but there was still no trip reset.

Many 1972 US specification V7 Sports had a silver-painted frame, with a red fuel tank and tool boxes. Others were green, lime green, or red with a black-painted frame. A side stand was optional but not recommended; spring-loaded, the side stand often self-retracted, leaving the expensive V7 Sport lying on its side. Although most of this US series was produced during 1972, examples were sold well into 1973.

Production V7 Sport 1973 (second series from frame number VK 13205- VK 13840)

According to the factory parts catalogue, the second series of production V7 Sport began at frame number VK 13205, and went through until frame number VK 13840. Production commenced in December 1972 (according to official service bulletins), presumably as 1973 models. As 1587 V7 Sports were produced during 1973 (including this and the more numerous third series with drum or disc brakes), a figure of around 635 seems reasonable for this series. Pre-assembled engines continued to be randomly fitted to a chassis, and the engine number sequence remained extremely inconsistent with the frame sequence. Engine numbers range from around VK 31800 to approximately VK 33447, overlapping considerably with the earlier 1972 series, and also with the later 1973 series. Some of this series was also fitted with engines later than frame number VK 33448 that included the third series revisions; again, it is easier to categorise this series by frame number. US examples continued with a foil over the frame number stating the VIN as the engine number, further complicating classification.

1972 US V7 Sports often featured a silver-painted frame. (Courtesy Moto Guzzi)

Gen	Neut		
	Lights	Oil	

For this series there were detail updates only to the engine, but considerably more to the transmission. The rocker shaft retaining bolts were increased in size from 12mm

The taillight was larger and the turn signals Lucas on 1972 US V7 Sports. (Courtesy Moto Guzzi)

Moto Guzzi Sport & Le Mans Bible

US V7 Sport distinguishing features 1972 and 1973

Identification tag on steering head
Many with a silver-painted frame
Veglia miles per hour speedometer
Dashboard lettering in English
CEV sealed beam headlight
Larger CEV taillight
Lucas turn signals

My early, second series V7 Sport VK 13209, with tank badges instead of decals. The engine number is VK 32666: this is one of the remaining few without a starter solenoid.

to 14mm; there was a new transmission case (still retaining external webbing); a new transmission cover, and a number of internal modifications. Along with updated steel bearing retaining plates now located by three screws instead of two, the first of a series of updated transmission layshafts was introduced. This included wider flanges for the thicker sleeves (5mm) between the layshaft and caged needle bearings under 1st, 2nd and 3rd gears. The earlier 3mm sleeves were known to fail and updated transmissions were stamped with a '4' next to the speedometer drive. The final drive drain plug was also magnetic.

The fuel tank decals and insignia on this series were also changed, with metal 'Moto Guzzi' badges generally replacing the earlier decals. Most examples of this series featured red and white decal stripes

200KPH & 200KG: THE V7 SPORT (1971-1973)

Many second series V7 Sports had these heavier section handlebars which continued into the third series.

above and below the badges, now spaced further apart. Colour choice increased with blue, bronze and black now available alongside red, green and lime green. The toolbox 'V7 Sport' decals were initially unchanged, but at some stage during this series there were new fuel tank and toolbox decals, the tank with a single, narrow dark stripe underneath the tank badges, and only a winged eagle decal on the toolboxes. There was considerable inconsistency about which set of colours and decals appeared on which motorcycle: green seemed to predominate for Europe, and many US examples were painted black.

Also new from frame number VK 13205 were the clip-on handlebars, with new, 8x50mm chrome bolts and nuts in internal threads. These handlebars were much heavier in section – and uglier than the earlier version. They were one of the first indications of cost-cutting although these 'bars were not consistently installed as some later bikes had the earlier bars and vice versa. The instrument panel also received updated isolating rubbers at this time; there were longer alternator retaining screws; new, high tension sparkplug leads, and a new ignition switch and steering lock support. Other ignition changes included new Marelli ignition points, condensers and springs. The rear brake was also updated with a new tie rod, and there were new Ferodo I/HG 1 rear brake shoes.

In some respects this series represented the end of an era, the final version produced before concessions were made with accountants and legislation in mind. The next production series would see cheaper solutions used in the engine design, and a left side gearshift to accommodate US requirements.

Production V7 Sport 1973 and 1975 (third series from frame number VK 14000)

Although SEIMM managed to revive Moto Guzzi, in December 1972 the company was sold to Argentinean-born Alejandro De Tomaso. De Tomaso already owned Benelli, and whilst he was quick to assert his control over Moto Guzzi, it was initially business as usual. It was soon apparent that De Tomaso wasn't particularly interested in the existing big twins, and was reported to have strolled through the V7 assembly lines brandishing an engraved Arab sword à la Lawrence of Arabia, screaming "No more stupid twins". De Tomaso's immediate action was to restrict research and development, and demand a reduction in production costs. By mid-1973, the V7 Sport was finally touched by this economic rationalisation.

As the third series differed in a number of important details from earlier versions, the frame number sequence was new. Although this frame number sequence doesn't appear in officially released figures, it certainly existed, and the updates are described in the parts list. This new series began at VK 14000, leaving a gap of 160 from the earlier VK 13000 series. As no official factory data exists, and most examples were destined for the US with a VIN engine number, it is difficult to ascertain the exact number of VK 14000 series machines produced. 1973 data, and the few available 1975 production figures, indicate just over 1000 VK 14000 series examples (including disc brake versions). Engine numbers continued the previous sequence, and whilst the engine updates were initiated from VK 33448, many later series chassis were fitted with earlier specification engines, and it follows that some later specification engines were also probably installed in earlier chassis.

Engine and transmission

Engine updates for this series began at number VK 33448, and included new crankcases. The sump plug was magnetic and, although many changes were incorporated, Moto Guzzi still omitted an oil filter. There were new nuts (not chrome-plated) for the transmission mount, and new main bearing flanges and oil seal. Most changes centred on replacement

---

V7 Sport distinguishing features (from frame number VK 13205-VK 13840 engine number VK 31800-VK 33447 approx)

Engine and transmission
Rocker shaft retaining bolts were increased to 14mm
New transmission case (no 14200211)
New transmission cover (no 14200811)
Wider flanges between the layshaft and caged needle bearings under 1st, 2nd and 3rd gears
New, three-screw transmission bearing retaining plates
Magnetic sump plug fitted in final drive housing
Marelli 71111601 and 71147601 ignition points
Marelli 7114690 and 71147010 ignition advance springs
Marelli 56181133 and 56181134 condensers
New high tension sparkplug leads
Longer alternator retaining screws

Chassis
Fuel tank gained metal 'Moto Guzzi' badges in place of the decals
Alternative fuel tank and tool boxes with new decals and wider range of colours
New instrument rubber supports
New heavier section adjustable handlebars
Updated steering lock and ignition switch support
New rear brake tie rod
Ferodo I/HG 1 rear brake shoes

The third series V7 Sport was characterized by a left side gearshift and rod-operated rear brake. Some continued with the same fuel tank and toolbox decals as the previous series. (Courtesy Moto Guzzi)

200KPH & 200KG: THE V7 SPORT (1971-1973)

of the camshaft timing gears with a chain. While this was undoubtedly a cost-cutting exercise, and did facilitate easier camshaft timing because there were no timing marks on the gears, it also introduced a new set of problems.

The drive included three sprockets (19 tooth at the crank, 38 tooth at the camshaft, and 34 tooth at the oil pump), and a duplex chain. There was a manual timing chain tensioner with a soft rubbing block that was problematic and often failed. The oil pump included a new body, new gears (a 24 tooth to replace the earlier 31 tooth), and a 12x22x20mm needle bearing on the oil pump shaft. Inside the gearbox was a new pre-selector, the clutch arm incorporated a bend to avoid contact with the transmission case if out of adjustment, and there was a new clutch cable. Earlier straight clutch arms could foul the transmission case if not correctly adjusted. There were a few updates to the ignition system, including new Marelli contact breakers, springs and condensers.

Chassis

Essentially, the chassis was as before, but there was some modification to the frame and fittings. New lower frame tubes had flattened rear connections to allow for new brake and gearshift support brackets. The revised lower tubes also required a new centre stand. In anticipation of new left side gearshift regulations coming into force in the US after September 1974, the gearshift and rear brake linkages were revised.

This new set-up featured on all post-VK 14000 chassis; an inferior gearshift solution compared to the earlier, cable-operated rear brake and Heim-jointed gearshift connection. The gearshift now operated via a 6mm threaded clevis pin and hooked rod, introducing slop into the shift, while the rear brake also operated through a rod with hook linkage. This set-up was also not as progressive as the earlier cable arrangement, and it was obviously a short term solution as the rear brake plate was unchanged, still with provision for the cable. As pre-assembled engine and transmission units were fitted in these chassis, the transmission shifting drum was also unchanged, still providing a one-up and four-down gearshift pattern. When moved to the left side, this pattern (opposite to other left shifting motorcycles) was maintained. As the shafts fitted full length behind the transmission, it was possible

A number of engine updates for the third series V7 Sport included a chain for the camshaft drive instead of gears. (Courtesy Two Wheels)

to move the gearshift back to the right and brake to the left as on earlier V7 Sports, although generally the bikes came from the factory shifting on the left.

With this revised gearshift and rear brake were new levers and rubbers, and new, forged steel footpeg supports with different frame mounts. Other chassis updates included installation of round reflectors on the front fork and rear mudguard (as on US versions), although, as with turn signals, fitting of these was inconsistent. This version also received a new wiring loom, and there were fewer chrome-plated fasteners. Some of the later bikes featured a chrome-plated Tommaselli throttle instead of the alloy Magura.

Although produced in 1973, the VK 14000 series of V7 Sport was sold mostly into 1974 as US versions. Not many examples of this series were readily available in the UK, and for 1974 there was a new distributor – Barrett, of Redhill, Surrey, which distributed the new 750 S in greater numbers than the V7 Sport.

V7 Sport disc brake
From 1973, disc brakes could always be specified as a factory option; either a double front disc or triple disc set-up. The Brembo triple disc arrangement featured on the prototype Premio Varrone Le Mans

Many of this final series had updated decals on the fuel tank and toolboxes. (Courtesy Two Wheels)

V7 Sport distinguishing features (from frame number VK 14000; engine number VK 33448-VK 34450 approx)

Engine and transmission
New crankcases
New nuts and washers for the transmission mount (no longer chrome-plated)
New main bearing flanges and seal
Magnetic sump plug fitted in crankcase
Camshaft and oil pump drive by duplex chain with manual tensioner
New oil pump body and gears (24 tooth)
12x22x20mm needle bearing on the oil pump shaft
New gearbox pre-selector
New dogleg clutch arm
New clutch cable
New contact breakers, springs and condensers

Chassis
New lower frame tubes with flattened rear points
Revised gearshift for left side shifting with new bracket
New forged steel footpeg brackets
New centre stand
Rod-operated rear brake for right side operation
Some examples had round reflectors fitted to front fork and rear mudguard
New wiring loom
Fewer chrome-plated fasteners
Some final examples with Tommaselli throttle

200KPH & 200KG: THE V7 SPORT (1971-1973)

Although some components were a lower specification, the style of the V7 Sport was unchanged for this series. (Courtesy Moto Guzzi)

Below: The final series of V7 Sport had identical performance to that of earlier examples, but was no longer class-leading. (Courtesy Two Wheels)

at the end of 1972, but this was a linked brake set-up. A small number (152) V7 Sports were produced in 1973 with a factory dual front disc brake, most destined for the US. In all other respects they were identical to the drum brake version. The disc front brake was considerably more effective, but the additional weight of the dual, cast-iron discs punished the softly-sprung front fork more severely. The twin disc braking system was really state-of-the-art for 1973, with dual 300mm, cast-iron discs and twin opposed piston 08 Brembo brake calipers. In 1973, no other production bike had a comparable braking system.

Along with new, polished aluminium fork legs that accepted forward-mounted Brembo calipers was a cast aluminium hub that accepted 40 straight pull spokes. The front wheel was still aluminium Borrani, but not the stronger section Cross Borrani previously used on the front, and also on the rear. The lip on the front Borrani rim was noticeably shallower than on the rear, and flared outward as was usual with lightweight racing Borrani rims of that period. The front master cylinder was a 15.9mm Brembo without a clear fluid reservoir. There was no change to the front tyre which remained a Michelin S41 3.25x18 inch. The twin disc kit offered by the factory (14 92 30 00) was primarily for the US market: it came beautifully packaged and was very comprehensive, including replacement fork legs, front mudguard stays – and even a replacement clutch lever and bracket to match the Brembo brake lever. Also available was a rear disc kit, including a 220mm disc and rear master cylinder. This was quite a rare option and could generally only be specified if the machine was collected at Mandello as factory installation was required.

Although a further 100 V7 Sports were built in 1975 for Berliner in America, these had disc front brakes, and were essentially the 750 S converted to look like a V7 Sport. The V7 Sport was always a very popular model in the US but Berliner was reluctant to import the new-look 750 S. This final series of V7 Sport also had 750 S-style tool boxes and the 750 S seat. After three years, production totalled 3843 units and, compared to other Italian sporting motorcycles of the time (Ducati 750 Sport and Super Sport and Laverda 750 SFC), this was a remarkably high number.

The V7 Sport firmly re-established Moto Guzzi as a leading producer of high quality sporting motorcycles, but in some respects was showing its age. Drum front brakes, even if they were four-leading shoe, were considered old-fashioned, and the V7 Sport styling was conservative. De Tomaso

Dual Brembo disc front brakes were offered as an option. This example (VK 13703) was one of the last second series V7 Sports, delivered at Mandello in 1973 with triple disc brakes.

A rear Brembo disc was a factory-fitted option on the V7 Sport.

had already instigated a regime of cost-cutting and restyling; by 1974, most Benellis and their Moto Guzzis clones were restyled, and the V7 Sport was next in line for a styling update.

While some claim the 850 Le Mans to be the archetypal sporting Moto Guzzi, in my view the earlier V7 Sport Telaio Rosso holds that position. As a pure, uncompromised, sporting motorcycle, the larger machine offered little over the original Telaio Rosso. The V7 Sport was built as the embodiment of an engineer's ideal, and not compromised by economics, fashion or marketing. The 850 Le Mans was a great motorcycle, and a stylistic triumph, but it was still designed to embody late 1970s styling fashions. As a pure example of form following function, the V7 Sport makes no such concession, and is the greatest sporting Moto Guzzi of the modern era.

Many final V7 Sports had a factory-fitted dual disc front brake.

200KPH & 200KG: THE V7 SPORT (1971-1973)

Lean and functional: the 1973 V7 Sport was one of the finest sporting motorcycles of the 1970s.

3 De Tomaso style: 750 S & 750 S3

The 750 S was an interim model, and, apart from styling, was similar to the disc brake 1973 V7 Sport. (Courtesy Moto Guzzi)

By early 1974, Alejandro De Tomaso stated his intention was to double Moto Guzzi production between 1975 and 1978. Optimistically envisaging production of 400,000 motorcycles, most of the increase was to come from clones of newly developed Benelli fours and two-strokes. There was some development to the existing Moto Guzzi twins but all eyes were on Benelli at this stage.

During 1973, De Tomaso received incredible publicity from the release of the new Benelli 750 Sei, overshadowing all other models, including the

DE TOMASO STYLE: 750 S & 750 S3

Moto Guzzi twins. The consensus at the time was that the existing Moto Guzzis – including the V7 Sport – were too conservative and old-fashioned. The V7 Sport's specification was also considered too high to be profitable. Not only was the double-sided, twin-leading shoe front brake obsolete, it was more expensive to produce than a comparable disc brake, while Tonti's special detail touches also added considerably to the cost.

While the development team was busy working on the new 850 T it also found time to create an interim Sport model, the 750 S. First shown at the Milan Show in November 1973, the 750 S replaced the V7 Sport and was homologated for production on 13 February 1974. Production began alongside the 850 T, but, whilst many new features were introduced on the T, most didn't make it to the 750 S. This seemed incongruous considering the 750 S was supposedly the range leader, but when asked about this by Ivar de Gier, Tonti replied: "De Tomaso was not interested in developing this model." Most Moto Guzzis produced in 1974 were 850 Ts, and this left the single year 750 S as an unusual model; a bridge between the old, where cost wasn't a consideration, and the new, with the emphasis on style.

750 S

The 750 S was very similar in specification to the 1973 disc-braked, VK 14000-series, V7 Sport but featured a new chassis number sequence. This began at VK1 11111, running to VK1 12315. As expected, there were always more frame numbers than bikes produced. Engine numbers continued the V7 Sport series, and, as the engine specification was essentially unchanged, there was some overlap of numbers with the V7 Sport. All 750 S engines had numbers after VK 33448, and included the updated cam chain and oil pump. Known engine numbers seemed to range from approximately VK 33700-VK35000.

Most 750 Ss had some transmission updates, but as transmissions were often assembled independently of engines, not all 750 Ss may have featured these modifications. There was a different 5th gear, with the same ratio as before but 28/21 teeth. The teeth were not as greatly angled – closer to straight cut – claiming to reduce 5th gear spline wear. The gearbox mainshaft was updated to include a caged needle bearing instead of the bronze thrust washer at the front. Shaft dimensions were also changed with this update. Also new was a reversed shifting drum, now providing a more usual left side one-down, four-up gearshift pattern. Accompanying this was a new gearshift detent mechanism, although the spring was unchanged, and a new rear transmission cover. The final drive was the same as the V7 Sport, but the oil filler plug was no longer chrome-plated, and included a magnet.

At some stage during the production run there were a few

Early 750 Ss still didn't include a solenoid above the starter motor. Three colour schemes were available. (Courtesy Moto Guzzi)

The Plexiglas fairing of the V7 Sport was still an option on the 750 S.

electrical system updates. Like early 850 Ts, the alternator was initially the V7 Sport 180 watt, but while the 850 T featured a solenoid for the electric start, this didn't initially appear on the 750 S. Lack of a solenoid was one of the V7 Sport's main problems, and the solenoid also doesn't feature in any of the early 750 S factory publicity pictures. During the production run the 750 S gained an 850 T starting set-up, with a solenoid mounted above

The 750 S instrument panel and handlebar controls were the same as on the V7 Sport.

As on the V7 Sport, the rear mudguard was hinged to allow the seat to flip upward. (Courtesy Two Wheels)

a more powerful (black-painted) Bosch DF-12V-0.6 horsepower motor. At the same time the alternator was uprated to a Bosch G1-14V-20A-21 280 watt, but it's not known when this changeover point occurred. Certainly, some late 1974 test bikes included a solenoid, and two Bosch starter motors are listed in the September 1974 parts catalogue (one with a solenoid). All other equipment was identical to the final series disc brake V7 Sport, including the electrical fuel tap on the left, CEV switches and round taillight, Veglia instruments with four-light panel, 45 watt CEV headlight, five-way ignition with lock, and the final V7 Sport-series adjustable handlebars.

On some 750Ss the dash panel was slightly different; still with four warning lights but these were a different type of bezel. The warning inscriptions (in Italian) were not decals but were incorporated in the dashboard, and there was no lip in front of the panel. The throttle was also a chrome-plated Tommaselli on some examples. The 750 S also retained the underseat courtesy light.

The front fork was the same (with 34.715mm tubes), the brakes were dual 300mm Brembo with a 15.9mm master cylinder, and the front wheel a WM2 Borrani as used on the disc brake V7 Sport. The Brembo master cylinder was the early type without a clear reservoir. The rear brake was also unchanged from the V7 Sport, including the boss on the outer plate for the previous brake cable. Considering the 850 T had a narrower rear brake and rubber cush drive, it appears that Moto Guzzi was still using existing parts stock when building the 750 S.

Most transitional changes from V7 Sport to 750 S were stylistic. By 1975, many Italian motorcycle manufacturers were investigating new stylistic ideas, and De Tomaso was at the forefront in this.

De Tomaso had a strong interest in automobiles, and the trend from automotive-inspired designers was a move away from round forms to the angular shapes that predominated in car design in the 1970s. The Benelli Sei began this trend, and Ducati followed by commissioning Giorgetto Giugiaro of Ital Design to design the angular 860 GT. As Moto Guzzi was busy developing the 850 T, fortunately, there was little it could do to the V7 Sport styling apart from introduce new colours and toolboxes. In hindsight, the angular shapes haven't stood the test of time, but the 750 S is now considered one of the best-looking motorcycles of the era, and represents Italian style at its best.

Because of bold styling initiatives the 750 S looked almost like a new motorcycle. The steel fuel tank also included metal 'Moto Guzzi' badges, and was painted black with a distinctive pair of diagonal stripes for which there were three colour choices: red, orange or green. These stripes continued to the 850 T-style lockable toolboxes (which also had metal badges) that extended beyond the rear frame downtube. The seat was a rather unusual one-and-a-half seat, similar in design to that which first appeared on the 'Premio Varrone' Le Mans at the end of 1972. Although this seat was not strictly a two-seater, the passenger footpegs were retained. While the Silentium mufflers were as before, they were painted matt black, attaching to the usual chrome-plated exhaust header pipes with the threaded head inserts, and the usual chrome-plated crossover pipe. The black paint was not particularly durable – even worse than the poor quality Italian chrome of the V7 Sport.

Other black touches were the black-painted steel footpeg and lever supports. Although the front forks were unchanged, the fork legs incorporated an eagle insignia rather than the earlier 'Moto Guzzi'.

Some 850 T improvements didn't extend to the 750 S. The 850 T received a rubber cush drive in the rear wheel, a significant improvement that virtually eliminated driveshaft spline wear, and also updated handlebar switches. The V1000 Convert and final series of 850 Ts also included the much needed spin-on automotive type oil filter and new sump. These 850 Ts were built in 1975, after the end of 750 S production, so these updates would wait until the 750 S3. Only 948 750 Ss were produced (compared to 5301 850 Ts), and it was essentially an interim model before the introduction of the 850 Le Mans. The 750 S sold in the UK for £1546.50, competing almost directly with the Benelli Sei from the same company, the exotic desmodromic Ducati 750 Super Sport, and Laverda 750 SFC. At the time a Honda 750 Four, Triumph Trident or Norton Commando sold for less than £1000, and expensive Italian 750s were really only for the connoisseur. Only a few Moto Guzzi 750 Ss were sold in the UK, but the Benelli, Ducati and Laverda fared no better. As with the V7 Sport, most 750 Ss were sold in Italy, Germany, France and the Netherlands. A small number were also sent to the US, but as Berliner was not particularly enthusiastic, most US 750 Ss were rebadged as V7 Sports (see previous chapter). Lino Tonti also exchanged his V7 Sport for a 750 S, fitting cast wheels, and a low, peculiar-looking seat, to suit his short stature.

Opposite: Long and low, the 750 S was a styling triumph.

As a functional sporting motorcycle, the 750 S continued the tradition of the V7 Sport. (Courtesy Two Wheels)

De Tomaso style: 750 S & 750 S3

750 S distinguishing features (from frame number VK 1 11111–VK 1 12315; engine number VK 33700 -VK 35000 approx)

New 5th gear with 28/21 teeth
Reversed gearshift drum
New gearshift detent mechanism
New rear transmission cover
Gearbox mainshaft updated to include a caged needle bearing at the front
Magnetic oil filler plug in final drive
During the production series the starter motor became a more powerful Bosch 0.6hp and gained aa solenoid
At this time the alternator became a Bosch 280 watt.
Dual 300mm Brembo front brakes with 15.9mm master cylinder without clear reservoir
WM2 Borrani 40-spoke alloy front wheel
Black paint on tank and toolboxes with red, green or orange stripes
Metal tank and toolbox badges
850 T-style lockable toolboxes
Black-painted forged steel footpeg brackets
Matt black Silentium mufflers
Fork legs incorporated an eagle insignia rather than the earlier 'Moto Guzzi'
Some instrument panels without front lip and different warning lights
Some with Tomaselli throttle

Moto Guzzi Sport & Le Mans Bible

750 S3

Although a final 100 V7 Sports were manufactured in 1975, these were 750 Ss built for the US market and rebadged as V7 Sports, and the end of Moto Guzzi's sporting 750 line was the 750 S3. The 850 Le Mans was already waiting in the wings, but delays in implementing production during 1975 meant the 750 continued for another year. The resulting 750 S3 was another confusing model, incorporating some improvements over the 750 S and V7 Sport, but generally reflecting the continual downgrading in specification and cost-cutting that typified the De Tomaso era.

The 750 S3 may have looked superficially similar to the 750 S, but was in most respects an inferior motorcycle. There were 55 modifications in parts specification between the 750 S and 750 S3. Many components of different models were incorporated and the 750 S3 was more closely related to the 850 T3 than the earlier 750 S. Some components were also inherited from the shortlived and ill-fated V1000 Convert automatic. The FMI (Federazione Motociclistica Italiana) homologation document of 21 September 1975 also shows a light-coloured half fairing on the bike, similar in shape to the upper half of the Imola 200 racing fairing, but with a headlight. This homologation example also included Dell'Orto PHF 36A 'pumper' carburettors as fitted to the later 850 Le Mans.

Three weeks prior to the homologation of the 750 S3 a production series racer was also homologated, but neither this racer nor the homologated 750S3 eventuated. Guzzi historian, Ivar de Gier, believes the 750 S3 was always intended to be something different – and a precursor to the 850 Le Mans – but instead became a victim of De Tomaso's programme of economic rationalisation. Tonti also told him that a Super Sport version of the 750 S3 was planned for 1975 if the production of the 850 Le Mans was stymied. It may have had deficiencies, but the 750 S3 was still a stunning-looking motorcycle, with timeless styling in the finest Italian tradition.

The FMI homologation document for the 750 S3 pictured a bike with a racing-style fairing and Dell'Orto PHM 36 carburettors. (Courtesy Ivar de Gier)

Engine and transmission

Instead of continuing the earlier 750 S engine for another year, in order to reduce production costs the 750 S3 engine was based on the touring 850 T3, and was essentially the same 844cc T3 motor with the shorter stroke 750 S crankshaft, and slightly smaller, higher compression 82.5mm pistons. Because the camshaft was the milder touring 850 T3 type, the 750 S3 suffered performance-wise compared to the earlier 750 S and V7 Sport. Despite the engine's close relationship with the 850 T3, engine numbers continued the V7 Sport series, from around VK 35000 to VK 36200.

One advantage of the 850 T3 cylinder head was that the exhaust header pipes now attached to the cylinder head with two studs instead of screwing directly into the head, eliminating the previous problem of the exhaust header pipes working loose. The valve sizes and combustion chamber shape were unchanged from the 750 S, as were the cylinder head covers and intake system of Dell'Orto VHB 30C carburettors and plenum chamber without an air filter. As the 750 S3 motor was essentially that of an 850 T3, the pushrod tunnels were further spaced, requiring new rockers. The rocker covers were the newer, four-finned type, also featuring on the V1000 Convert and 850 T3, with the vents attached by banjo fittings. Additionally, the engine included a new front thrust bearing, changed from a bronze bush to a caged needle-type.

Although claimed power was unchanged at 70 horsepower at 7000rpm, the 750 S3 produced less power than the earlier 750 S and V7 Sport because of the milder 850 T3 camshaft. The inlet valve opened 20 degrees before top dead centre, closing 52 degrees after bottom dead centre, and the exhaust

De Tomaso style: 750 S & 750 S3

valve opened 52 degrees before bottom dead centre, closing 20 degrees after top dead centre. Inlet and exhaust valve lift was 6.58mm. Some later 750 S3s also had a lighter flywheel, shared with the new Le Mans, with the same timing marks as the 850T (2-33 degrees advance). These S3s featured the lower performance Marelli S311B distributor with a revised advance curve, which also contributed to performance loss.

All 750 S3s included a disposable oil filter in the sump as on the 850 T3 and final 850 T. The sump was attached by Allen bolts rather than hex head, and the fins on the pan were more rounded. Although undoubtedly beneficial for longer engine life, location of the oil filter inside the sump made replacement unnecessarily awkward and time-consuming, another design problem that Moto Guzzi refused to rectify under De Tomaso ownership. Sump capacity was also reduced slightly, to 3 litres. The exhaust system included the matt black Silentium mufflers of the 750 S, with chrome-plated header pipes and the same crossover underneath the transmission. Because of the exhaust retaining studs in the cylinder heads, the header pipes were unique to the S3.

There were a number of clutch and transmission updates for the 750 S3. Inside the clutch was a new inner clutch body and clutch output shaft, along with an updated transmission layshaft, and 1st, 2nd, 3rd and 4th gear selectors and sleeves. There was also a new shifting drum and spring, and a magnetic transmission oil filler plug. First introduced on the V1000 Convert was a new final drive housing that would continue until 1993 on all sporting Moto Guzzis with a rear disc brake. A more angular casting, this was 2mm longer, with a shorter right fork, larger bearing, and a U-joint integral with the driveshaft. The volume of oil was reduced to 0.025 litres. The 750 S3 also received the 850 T3 final drive (7/33), and the rubber cush drive in the rear wheel, introduced with the 850T. This was an improvement, limiting shock loads through the drive train and reducing spline wear between the rear drive, driveshaft coupling, and transmission.

Chassis

The 750 S3 received a new frame number sequence, beginning at VK 2 15000 and finishing at VK 2 15998. Although the frame number sequence was new for the 750 S3, apart from brackets for the rear brake master cylinder (located under the right side toolbox cover), and small details like provision for a steering lock on the steering head, the frame was much the same as that of the 750 S. The Neiman steering lock – similar to that fitted to other Italian motorcycles – replaced the problematic plate lock. There was a new centre stand, new seat (although a similar 1½ seater style), and new side covers. These were no longer lockable and didn't include a toolbox as there wasn't space for one behind the rear master cylinder and electrics. As on the 850 T3, the toolkit was placed in a plastic tray that sat above the battery under the seat. The side covers also included specific '750-S3' metal badges and were reshaped from the 750 S. While the steel fuel tank

Another interim model, the 750 S3 looked similar to the 750 S but had a more mildly tuned engine. (Courtesy Moto Guzzi)

shape went unchanged, the fuel filler cap position was reversed, opening towards the rider (all later V7 Sport replacement fuel tanks featured this filler cap set-up). The solenoid-operated fuel tap on the left was also replaced by a manual tap. Although the 750 S and 750 S3 looked similar, most 750 S3 body components were new, including the front and rear mudguards and stays, and rear lifting handles. The rear mudguard retained the hinge for seat lifting. Standard were chrome-plated engine protection bars.

It was the braking system that really set apart the S3 from the earlier 750 S and V7 Sport. This featured the linked braking system pioneered on the Premio Varrone Le Mans of 1972, first seen in production on the V1000 Convert early in 1975. Tonti's linked brakes went back to the 1950s, to the mechanical linkage set-up on the Dama scooter, while Moto Guzzi had also experimented with them on the ill-fated 500cc, four-cylinder racer. Tonti attempted to install a mechanical linked braking system on the V7 also, but this proved too complex. With the introduction of hydraulic disc brakes, Umberto Todero continued development, working with Brembo in nearby Milan to create a braking system where the rear wheel locked first under all conditions. This early system didn't include a proportioning valve to provide more force to the front wheel; instead, featuring a simple, four-way manifold to split the fluid evenly from the rear master cylinder to the front and rear discs.

Although Todero wanted all braking to operate from the front lever, the German regulatory body, TüV, required separate controls for the front and rear brakes. The eventual system used was the handlebar-mounted 12.7mm front master cylinder connected to the right front 08 Brembo brake caliper, and a rear 15.875mm master cylinder operating the rear caliper and left front disc from the right foot pedal. The front brakes were twin 300mm discs, as on the 750 S, with a 242mm rear disc. This patented braking system was to become a Moto Guzzi trademark, featuring on all the other Moto Guzzis covered in this book.

The front fork stayed the same but for new, lower spring cups, and there was more oil per leg (0.070 litres). Controlling the rear end were Italian Sebac rear shock absorbers and springs. Built in Bologna, these were inferior units compared to the earlier Konis. The front wheel rim was now a wider WM3/2.15-18/40 RM-01-4745. Because of the rear disc set-up, the front and rear alloy Borrani wheel rims were similar 40-spoke WM3, but the Michelin S41 tyres were as before. Other 750 S3 updates included unique headlight mounting brackets, and non-adjustable, forward offset, black clip-on handlebars. Along with more forward-mounted 850 T3 footpegs (no longer with black-painted supports), these handlebars gave an awkward riding position. The headlight remained a weak 40/45 watt CEV, now with black-painted instead of chrome-plated shell, and the hydraulic steering damper was retained.

For the 750 S3 there were a number

The 750 S3 featured a new instrument panel and handlebar switches.

Standard on the 750 S3 were chrome-plated engine protection bars.

of updates to the electrical system, instruments and switches. Because it no longer incorporated a steering lock, the ignition switch was only three-position instead of four. All 750 S3s had the larger, 280 watt alternator and 0.6 horsepower Bosch starter motor with solenoid mounted above it. The starter with solenoid carried a new part number and included a clutch lever-operated cut-out switch. While the Veglia instruments were the same size, the faces were modernized, with fewer graduations, and the rims black instead of chrome. The dashboard and instrument surrounds were black, the gauges in rubber sleeves, and there was a new warning light display which included warnings for lights, main beam, generator, and oil pressure. There was still no trip reset and the gauges included winged eagle logos. As all 750 S3s were fitted with Aprilia turn signal indicators, it was surprising this new dashboard didn't include indicator lights. New plastic handlebar switches came from the 850 T3, including an ignition stop and starter on the right and turn signals on the left. These switches were more modern, and with the wires routed inside the handlebars the wiring looked tidier but was more difficult to repair if an electrical fault arose. Unlike the V7 Sport and 750 S there was only one start switch, no longer with a back-up activated by the ignition switch and now only through the handlebar switch. The throttle assembly was a chrome-plated Tommaselli Daytona 2C, with a throttle stop on the top. Continuing the updates was a new taillight, a larger CEV along the lines of that fitted to US V7 Sports.

With an increase in dry weight to 208kg (230kg wet), a reduction in real horsepower, and the higher final drive ratio, S3 performance suffered in comparison with the V7 Sport and other sporting motorcycles of 1975. Some contemporary road tests – with disappointing timed top speeds – were unflattering about this. *Motor Cycle,* in December 1975, managed a mean top speed of 114.21mph (184kph), with a standing start quarter mile time of 14.7 seconds at only 93.1mph (150kph). *Bike* magazine, testing the same machine also in December 1975, achieved a more respectable 123.45mph (199kph).

Total production was 950, and again, there were

more frame numbers than motorcycles built. UK distribution also changed in May 1975, coinciding with the release of the 750 S3. Coburn & Hughes, already a Ducati distributor, now handled Moto Guzzi, and the price of the 750 S3 was £1749. Although production had ended, the 750 S3 remained available into 1976. It was rumoured that up to 200 750 S3s were sold in the UK; if this figure is correct, a large proportion of the total production ended up in Britain.

By 1975 the 750 S3 was outclassed in outright performance, not only by larger capacity Italian machines, but also a new generation of German and Japanese Superbikes. The early 1970s era of the 750 was over as buyers demanded more power and torque. Ducati's 750 Super Sport grew to a 900, the Laverda 750 SF usurped by the 1000cc triple, and the BMW and Kawasaki 900s were about to become 1000cc. Moto Guzzi had the 850 Le Mans waiting and ready to go, and now was the time to unleash it. While the 750 S3 was a beautiful and appealing motorcycle, compared to the earlier V7 Sport and 750 S it was flawed. After only one year it was eclipsed by the next landmark sporting Moto Guzzi, the 850 Le Mans, which heralded a new line of illustrious sporting machines.

The triple disc linked braking system set the 750 S3 apart from earlier 750 Sports. (Courtesy Moto Guzzi)

De Tomaso style: 750 S & 750 S3

750 S3 distinguishing features (from frame number VK 2 15000-VK 2 15998; engine number VK 35000-VK 36200 approx)

Different intake and exhaust valves
New rockers
850 T3 cylinder head casting with bolt exhaust header attachment
New four-finned rocker covers
New oil breather tubes for rocker covers attached by banjo fittings
850 T3 camshaft
Marelli S311B distributor
Disposable oil filter in sump
Sump retained by Allen bolts
Some later S3s with lighter flywheel
New outer clutch plate and clutch cable
New inner clutch body
New clutch shaft
New layshaft
New 1st, 2nd, 3rd and 4th gear selectors and sleeves
New gearshift drum and spring
Magnetic transmission oil filler plug
New final drive housing (2mm longer)
Convert-style U-joint integral with driveshaft
8/33 (4.714:1) final drive
Rubber cush drive in rear wheel
Larger rear drive bearing
Updated swingarm to accommodate longer final drive housing and U-joint
New centre stand
Chrome-plated engine protection bars installed
Front fork included new lower cup springs
New Sebac rear shock absorbers and springs
Wider Borrani WM3/2.15-18/40 RM-01-4745 front wheel
New rear lifting handle
Fuel tank cap opened towards rider
No electric fuel tap
Metal tank and side cover badges
New side covers
Neiman steering head lock
New headlight brackets
Black-painted headlight shell
Larger CEV taillight
New front and rear mudguards
12.7mm front master cylinder connected to the right front 08 Brembo brake caliper
15.875mm master cylinder linked to 242mm rear and left front caliper
Non-adjustable forward offset clip-on handlebars
New rear wheel and hub
New Bosch starter with solenoid

continued overleaf

Moto Guzzi Sport & Le Mans Bible

750 S3 distinguishing features (from frame number VK 2 15000-VK 2 15998; engine number VK 35000-VK 36200 approx)
continued

Three-position ignition switch
New Veglia instruments with different faces and black surrounds
Updated black plastic warning light display
Tommaselli Daytona 2C throttle
New plastic handlebar switches
More forward-mounted 850 T3 footpegs
850 T3 footpeg supports not painted black
Tool kit in plastic tray under the seat

Style with speed: the 850 Le Mans (1975-78)

In 1975 Alejandro De Tomaso was still gripped by multi-mania, and committed to producing the blatant Honda-cloned Benelli and Moto Guzzi fours. Well connected and politically powerful, De Tomaso successfully lobbied the Italian parliament to levy a tax on all under-380cc motorcycles imported from Japan. But even in the heavily protected domestic market, the Benelli and Moto Guzzi multis were considered expensive, lower quality, overweight Honda copies.

De Tomaso also purchased Maserati in 1975, transferring all research and development, sales, exports and administration to this facility at Modena. Benelli was now building all of the cycle parts for motorcycles at Pesaro. While De Tomaso was devoted to the fours and sixes, at Mandello the Moto Guzzi twin continued. Conservative Moto Guzzi buyers rejected the Benelli-built 350 and 400cc fours, and Moto Guzzi was rejuvenated by the release of the 850 T. Placing a touring engine in Tonti's 750 Sport frame proved highly successful, and 5086 850 Ts rolled out of the Mandello factory in 1974. This gave the twin a new lease of life – and was fortuitous for De Tomaso.

Despite the success of the 850 T, De Tomaso was not convinced there was a future for a sporting Moto Guzzi V-twin. He misguidedly envisaged that the Benelli 750 Sei would become Italy's premier sporting motorcycle, and wanted it rebadged as a Moto Guzzi. Although De Tomaso preferred that Guzzi did not manufacture twins at all, he was prepared to sanction development of the 850 T and automatic V1000 Convert. De Tomaso could see no sense in pursuing the path begun with the V7 Sport but, fortunately, Lino Tonti and his engineering department persuaded him otherwise. The resulting Le Mans became an iconic Moto Guzzi that would pass through various incarnations over the next 18 years to evolve into a new symbol of the marque.

850 Le Mans development

The idea for an 844cc twin began back in 1971 whilst the factory was initiating the V7 Sport. Jan Kampen in Holland built an 810cc racer for the Zandvoort six-hour race using Volkswagen pistons, and this engine proved exceptionally torquey and smooth-running. Kampen and Tonti were in regular communication, and Tonti used racing as a means of acquiring development funding from the management.

Tonti decided to concentrate on an 850cc unit for the factory racers in non-production classes and above 750cc, and began work on an 844 based on the V7 Sport. Ivar de Gier interviewed both Tonti and Kampen and says: "This was an era of intense co-operation between the two, sharing of parts and ideas. Two 844cc prototypes were built, and they each received one for development. The camshaft was that of the V7 Sport, advanced ten degrees, to prevent fuel blowbacks from the 36 mm carburetors. This engine featured Fath valve springs and delivered 76 horsepower. Kampen had unlimited use of the University of Delft test bench, and the aid of Paul Klaver, a combustion engine specialist at the University. Soon his 850 engine delivered more power than Tonti's. Kampen tested 65 exhaust systems, perfecting it incrementally, and Tonti commissioned Lafranconi to build it. This was later to become the Lafranconi aftermarket Le Mans exhaust system, complete with distinctive swirls they later added themselves." Kampen and Klaver built many cylinder heads, using a variety of valve sizes, sharing the best with Tonti.

While development of the 850 was under way, Tonti produced some examples of a special V7 Sports as an entry in the 'Premio Varrone' design award at the end of 1972. This machine, titled the 'Le Mans', provided an interesting glimpse of the future sporting Moto Guzzi. Though based on a production V7 Sport (with die-cast crankcase and transmission castings, but a black-painted Telaio Rosso frame), it included a number of new features. Measuring 844cc (83x78mm) as on the Le Mans racers, carburation was via a pair of Dell'Orto PHM 40mm carburettors on straight intake manifolds. Power was a claimed 82 horsepower at 7500rpm, but the engine was mildly tuned, with a standard exhaust system and Lafranconi mufflers. The electric start also included a starter solenoid, which wouldn't appear on the sporting Guzzi twin until sometime during 1974.

The final drive was an earlier Telaio Rosso casting, still with the 8/35 ratio, providing a standing 400 metres in 12.25 seconds and a top speed of 225kph. While the weight of 206kg was unchanged from the V7 Sport, the Le Mans featured triple disc brakes and Borrani alloy wheels fitted with larger Michelin tyres; a 3.50x18 on the front and a 4.25x18 on the rear. The brakes were twin 300mm discs on the front and a 240mm on the rear, with new Brembo 08 twin-piston brake calipers. The rear master cylinder was crudely attached to the rear subframe on the left. The triple disc brakes were also linked as on the later 750 S3 (described in the previous chapter). Styling alterations included a frame-mounted half fairing similar to that on the Bol d'Or bikes, and an abbreviated humpback seat (which appeared on the later 750 S and S3).

The 'Premio Varrone' bikes represented a minor interlude, as behind the scenes Tonti was still developing the 850 as a racing machine which culminated in the machine that was prepared for the Barcelona 24-hour race in June 1973. The new 850 managed 5th place only, not really suited to the tight Montjuich circuit, although the post-race strip down at Mandello showed the machine had stood up well to the rigours of the race. Tonti told the management that development of the 850 sports machine was complete, and asked for permission to start making production technical drawings. This was refused as De Tomaso wanted Benelli to spearhead his

The 'Premio Varrone' 850 Le Mans had a fairing similar to that on the endurance racing machines. (Courtesy Ivar de Gier)

The rear brake on the 'Premio Varrone' 850 was a disc. (Courtesy Ivar de Gier)

Above: Despite 40mm carburettors, the 'Premio Varrone' 850 was mildly tuned. (Courtesy Ivar de Gier)

Gazzola testing an early Le Mans prototype during 1973. This was still based on a V7 Sport, and had a rear drum brake. (Courtesy Ivar de Gier)

sporting line-up, and Tonti was assigned to "cost-cutting research," which resulted in the 750 S and 750 S3.

By 1974, De Tomaso could see that his Benellis were not the revolution he envisaged and lost interest in motorcycle production, no longer caring whether Benelli or Moto Guzzi built a sports motorcycle, which provided Tonti with another opportunity to initiate production of the 850 Le Mans. Tonti's problem now was budgetary, and he was forced to base the 850 Le Mans engine on that of the 750 S3. When the Le Mans specification was finalised and prepared for production, the racing engines also evolved from V7 Sport-based to 750 S3-based. The eventual production 850 Le Mans engine would be an amalgam of components developed for the V7 Sport and 750 S3.

Gazzola testing one of the early 850 Le Mans prototypes during 1974. It has a later final drive, sump extension, black valve covers, and new exhaust system. (Courtesy Ivar de Gier)

850 Le Mans 1975-76 (first series; from frame number VE 11111-VE 13040)

Now considered one of the classic Moto Guzzis, the Le Mans also represents the archetypal, late 1970s sporting motorcycle. In the early 1970s, the Italian motorcycle industry was at the forefront of the Superbike revolution, its 750s setting the standard for engine and chassis performance. By 1975, Superbike requirements had changed, with the emphasis on larger displacement motors, more ergonomic controls, and stylistic features that were not necessarily functional. The move to larger displacement engines was primarily to maintain performance in the wake of increased noise level regulations. Whereas early 1970s Italian motorcycles were all about function, towards the end of the decade style predominated.

The Le Mans was really remarkably similar to the 750 S3, but a triumph of style and design. Many late 1970s and early 1980s motorcycle designs haven't stood the test of time, but the 850 Le Mans was a styling miracle. Instead of following the fashion of angular shapes and over-stylized forms, the Le Mans retained strong links with the earlier V7 Sport. The 850 Le Mans was first displayed at the Milan Show in November 1975, and was always known simply by this name. At a later stage some commentators began calling it the Mark 1, but this is incorrect; as far as all official literature and the factory is concerned, the first 850 Le Mans was simply that: the 850 Le Mans, which was also unusual in that production commenced prior to the Milan Show and the model was available as soon as it was shown. The Le Mans received a new frame number series, beginning at VE 11111. The first series finished sometime during 1976, at frame number VE 13040, indicating production of around 1929 motorcycles. Moto Guzzi figures show that Le Mans production numbered

Gazzola on one of the final prototypes at the Bol d'Or in 1975. This had a dual seat, and the heavy, metal side cover badges had red lettering – but still no fairing. (Courtesy Ivar de Gier)

219 in 1975 and 695 through until May 31 1976. Of these, only 84 went to the US. The Le Mans also received considerable publicity, and was test ridden by Giacomo Agostini for the Italian magazine, *La Moto*, in June 1976.

Engine and transmission

The basic architecture of the Le Mans engine was inherited from the 850 T3, and there were surprisingly few special internal parts. Like the chassis, Le Mans engines were identified by a VE prefix before the engine number, with engine numbers beginning at around VE 70000. US bikes continued to use

Giacomo Agostini tested the Le Mans during 1976 for an Italian motorcycle magazine. (Courtesy Ivar de Gier)

The 850 Le Mans was spectacularly styled and has become a seventies icon. (Author's collection)

the engine number for VIN identification. The performance boost over the 750 S3 came from the cylinder head, higher compression ratio, larger displacement, and bigger carburettors breathing through velocity stacks.

The camshaft was the same as that of the 750 S3 and 850 T3, with mild timing and 6.8mm of intake valve lift, while the combustion chamber was modified to incorporate larger 44mm inlet and 37mm exhaust valves. To make room for the larger valves, the combustion chamber volume was increased; now 74mm (up from 71mm), with a depth of 27mm, and a wide squish band to aid turbulence. The valve stems were still 8mm; the valves were supported by 52mm guides and operated by lighter pushrods.

To achieve a compression ratio of 10.2:1, the 83mm pistons had a much higher dome and, unlike the 850 T with its chrome-plated cylinders, the Le Mans featured cast-iron liners. The thinner piston rings of the 850 T were used on the Le Mans, but there were now only three: two compression (1.48mm), and an oil scraper (3.98mm). The high-domed pistons improved performance, but cylinder flame propagation was inferior. As a result the Le Mans engine was prone to detonation and running hot. Although the stroke was lengthened on the 850, the con-rods remained the same at 140mm, providing a slightly less than perfect 1.79:1 stroke to con-rod length ratio. The shorter rods increased piston acceleration, but also boosted low end torque.

The Le Mans had a thinner and lighter flywheel, too (reduced from 12 to 8mm), and new clutch plates with a different friction material. Earlier testing by Jan Kampen in Holland had shown that the flywheel would fail if it was thinner than 8mm, information he shared with Tonti.

Complementing the higher compression and bigger valves were Dell'Orto PHF 36B carburettors mounted on rubber manifolds, with open bell mouths. On early examples these bell mouths had wire gauze. Distinguishing the Le Mans from the 850 T3 were smaller (6mm rather than 8mm) manifold nuts.

The 36mm carburettors also featured accelerator pumps, now an improved diaphragm type, and a side pull mechanism operating the slide through a polished aluminium top bell crank. This allowed

Inside the Le Mans engine were a number of higher performance components. The air filters were not standard as the large Dell'Orto carburettors originally breathed through open bell mouths.

Style with speed: the 850 Le Mans (1975-78)

for a quick-acting throttle, but with a stronger stroke than even the square-slide Dell'Orto (always noted for its heavy action). The carburettors also included a choke, operated by a pair of cables connecting to a lever next to the left fuel tap. On the very first carburettors the aluminium float bowls were polished, and the banjos aluminium.

One of the most noticeable updates was a new exhaust system. Painted matt black to complement existing styling, this featured single-walled, 40 mm header pipes, with a balance pipe across the front of the engine, underneath the alternator. There was a second balance pipe underneath the transmission, but this was no longer a double crossover as on the V7 Sport. The mufflers were upswept, and – while still very quiet – were also very efficient. The main problem with the exhaust system was that the black paint wasn't very durable, and rusted prematurely. The five-speed transmission was as before but for a stronger gearshift return spring, constructed of 3.2mm wire with three coils instead of two. There was also an improved oil seal for the transmission input shaft, with a serrated lip seal instead of the smooth item as used on the output shaft. Another oil seal improvement was an O-ring fitted between 5th gear on the layshaft and the output bearing in the rear transmission cover.

Unlike the T3 (and later S3), the distributor was the Marelli S311A of the earlier 750 Sport, but provided only 34 degrees of full ignition advance as there were fewer degrees of static advance. The starter motor (with solenoid) and alternator were the same as on the final 750 S3, and, while early starter motors were painted silver, most were painted black. To save weight Moto Guzzi installed a smaller, 20 Ah battery on the Le Mans which struggled to power the motor in adverse conditions. Claimed power for the Le Mans was 80 horsepower (SAE) at 7300rpm, but this was optimistic. Standard Le Mans gearing was as for the S3, with 17/21 primary and 7/33 final drive, although some Le Mans were fitted from the factory with a close ratio, straight-cut racing gearbox. These gearboxes were distinguished by a ZD (instead of the usual T) prefix behind the starter motor on the battery plate boss. Also carried over from the S3 was the updated final drive.

Chassis

Like the engine, the Le Mans chassis was also quite similar to that of the 750 S3. Sharing the same dimensions, the frame was painted satin black and retained the removable lower tubes. Many 750 S3 features continued, such as the Neiman steering head lock and rear brake master cylinder under the right side cover. The twin ignition coils were located under the left side cover and the toolkit in a plastic tray above the battery. The two-position LISPA hydraulic steering damper was still adjusted by a knob on the steering head.

While the 34.715mm cartridge front fork, still with a 180mm fork width, appeared outwardly similar to that of the 750 S3, it was unique to the Le Mans. To save weight, fork tube walls were thinner and the fork included a different threaded, round Allen-headed fork nut instead of a hexagonal nut that provided more spring preload. Fork oil capacity was increased to 0.120 litres per leg, and early Le Mans had polished aluminium lower fork legs. A pair of 320mm LISPA shock absorbers controlled the rear end.

Following fashion trends the functional and light alloy Borrani rims made way for heavier cast alloy FPS wheels, still with the same WM3 rim sizes (2.15x18 inch). With 12 angled spokes, these silver-painted wheels included six-bolt disc mounts.

5mm cartridge fork, it had FPS cast alloy wheels instead of the Borrani wire-spoked type.

Standard tyres were Metzeler Rille 10 on the front and C7 Block Racing on the rear. Similar Metzeler tyres were also fitted to the Ducati Super Sport of 1974 and 1975, and on both the Ducati and Le Mans they were unsatisfactory, giving a slippery and greasy feel; there were certainly better tyre options available in 1975 and 1976, notably the new Pirelli MT18 series.

The Le Mans also featured the integrated braking system of the 750 S3 with the same four-way manifold located on the left rear downtube. Braking was by Brembo 08 calipers as before, with two drilled 300mm front discs and one 242mm rear disc, and the same size master cylinders. The Brembo brake calipers included twin bleeder valves and the rear caliper bracket was shared with the V1000 Convert, still incorporating the drilled and tapped bosses for a rear parking brake. To reduce unsprung weight, the front cast-iron discs featured aluminium carriers. The front master cylinder also included a clear reservoir. These brakes were extremely effective, and certainly amongst the best available in 1975 and 1976. Unlike tyre choice, Moto Guzzi's brake pad selection was more appropriate: Ferodo/Ferrit 332 GG for the right front and rear calipers, and Ferrit 330 FF on the left front caliper.

Style

But the Le Man's raison d'être was more about style than performance. During the mid-1970s, the factory café racer was seen by many European manufacturers as a way of countering the threat of cheaper, faster, and continually improving Japanese motorcycles. BMW began the trend at the end of 1973 with its ground-breaking R90S; Norton followed with the John Player 850 of 1974, and in 1976 Ducati decided to put its limited edition 900 Super Sport into regular production. Even Harley-Davidson followed suit in 1977 with the XLCR.

But none of these was such a successful stylistic creation as the Le Mans. The Le Mans may have suffered from marginal execution and indifferent quality, but more than any other motorcycle epitomizes the mid- to late 1970s café racer style. And unlike other deliberately styled motorcycles – in particular the Benelli fours and six and the Ducati 860 GT – the Le Mans has stood the test of time.

While the red or blue-grey painted steel fuel tank was the same shape as that on the 750 S3, side covers and front and rear mudguards were plastic. The fuel tank and side cover badges were also metal, but not heavy steel with red lettering as on one prototype. Side cover emblems were highlighted in black. Produced by Gaman, the moulded rubber seat was new, covering the rear of the tank. More angular-shaped than the S3, this seat looked impressive but was poorly made, and the rubber foam split early on. The final prototype tested by Gazzola at the Bol d'Or in September 1975 featured a foam dual seat, similar to the second series Le Mans, which also split and was replaced for production by the one-and-a-half person foam seat. Unfortunately, this also split and most first series Le Mans seats were replaced under warranty.

The seat was also hard and slippery; a triumph of styling over function. The rear mudguard no longer hinged to allow the seat to fold back as the mudguard and taillight were attached to the seat, folding down with it. Height range was limited by the clearance between the registration plate holder and tyre. Complementing the aggressive riding position was a small fairing encompassing the 40/45 watt headlight. Although the early prototypes didn't include the fairing, it was included later to give a more modern look. More stylistic than functional, the fairing had a day-glow orange panel on the front, and US examples featured a sealed beam headlight,

Setting apart the Le Mans from other sporting motorcycles was the small headlight fairing with DayGlo panel.

The original one-and-a-half person seat on the Le Mans was extremely problematic.

which jutted out, slightly spoiling the lines. Although not indicated as a different part in official parts lists, the US fairing had a larger hole to accommodate this headlight.

The instruments, instrument panel, handlebar switches and hand grips were inherited from the 750 S3, as were the forward-mounted, clip-on handlebars and CEV taillight. The taillight bracket was incorporated in the rear mudguard moulding. As on the S3, Veglia instruments were ridiculously optimistic, the speedometer didn't include a trip meter and the instruments (with winged eagle logo) were encased by rubber sleeves. The tachometer read to 8000rpm with a redline from 7250rpm (as on the 750 S3). The handlebar switch wires were still routed through the handlebars, and on early examples the throttle was a chrome-plated Tommaselli Daytona 2C, with a throttle stop screw on the top (soon changed to a black chrome-type with the throttle stop screw underneath). The horn was a single Voxbell. Many components were finished in black, including the CEV turn signal bodies, clutch and brake levers, lifting handle on the left connecting to the brake manifold, and tubular steel footpeg supports. (The cheap footpeg supports were typical of the cost-cutting that would become even more prevalent as the years went by, and also gave a different riding position to that of the earlier 750, with the footpegs lower and further forward: 70mm below and 88mm in front of the swingarm pivot.

An optional racing uprating kit was available for the Le Mans which included a set of straight-cut, close ratio gears, and a choice of two primary ratios (16 and 17 teeth). Also available were four different final drive ratios (6/32, 7/33, 8/33, 9/34), giving an amazing selection of alternative overall gear ratios. Other items in the racing kit included Dell'Orto PHM 40 carburettors, a B10 higher lift camshaft (7.2mm of intake valve lift), megaphone exhaust system, and a 24 litre aluminium fuel tank. There was also a set of washers to tighten the valve springs. It wa necessary to enlarge the intake and exhaust ports to 36.5mm.

At the premium price of £1999 in 1976, the Le Mans continued the trend begun with the Telaio Rosso. Although no longer the most expensive machine on the market (that distinction now went to the MV Agusta 750S America), it was still double the price of a Japanese 750. But the Le Mans style

The instrument panel and handlebar switches on the early Le Mans came from the 750 S3.

The first series Le Mans had the taillight housing incorporated in the rear mudguard.

caused a sensation, and, whilst not offering a huge performance increase compared to the V7 Sport, it was decidedly quicker than the 750 S3. In June 1976, *Motor Cycle News* achieved a top speed of 128.205mph (206kph), and *Bike* magazine an impressive 132.15mph (213kph) in August 1976.

The Le Mans was the right bike at the right time, offering similar performance to the Ducati 900 SS and Laverda 1000 3C in a civilised and compact package. Although the finish and quality of some items – notably the headlight and handlebar switches – was criticised, Tonti's magnificent frame was still more than up to the task, and the Le Mans remained one of the best-handling motorcycles available. With its excellent integral Brembo braking system, it was hard to find a better balanced all-round sporting motorcycle. Like the V7 Sport, the Le Mans was a class-leading machine – and it had the looks to match. One of the great sporting motorcycles of the mid- to late 1970s, the Le Mans was a masterpiece.

850 Le Mans 1977-78 (second series; frame number VE 13041-VE 17311)

For the second series, with production probably beginning around September 1976 after the summer break, updates were minor. Frame numbers continued from VE 13041 until VE 17311, while engine numbers also continued the VE series, from around VE 72000, finishing at around VE 76000. There does seem to be

Left: One area of obvious cost-cutting was the tubular steel footpeg brackets.

Handsome and timeless from any angle; the 1976 850 Le Mans in rare blue-grey. Lafranconi mufflers are from the optional race kit.

some discrepancy between the frame numbers and actual production figures, and the published frame numbers may be incorrect. At one stage the official frame number list omitted the series from VE 13041. Certainly, total production of 7036 units would indicate frame numbers beyond VE 17311, but these may not include US versions. Changes for this series were cosmetic only: all Le Mans now came with a black chrome Tommaselli Daytona 2C throttle, the carburettor float bowls were unpolished, and there

The 850 Le Mans also had real Superbike performance in 1976. (Courtesy Two Wheels)

STYLE WITH SPEED: THE 850 LE MANS (1975-78)

850 Le Mans distinguishing features first series (from frame number VE 11111-VE 13040)
Cylinder head received larger valves (44mm intake and 37mm exhaust)

- Lighter pushrods
- Three-ring 10.2:1 pistons
- Inlet manifolds attached by three 6mm bolts
- Dell'Orto PHF 36B carburettors with polished float bowls
- Bell mouths with wire gauze
- Early carburettor banjos aluminium; later, plastic
- Choke operated by lever near left fuel tap
- 40mm matt black exhaust system
- Black exhaust header retainers
- Clutch plate with new friction material
- New gearshift return spring
- New serrated lip seal for transmission input shaft
- O-ring fitted between 5th gear on the layshaft and rear bearing
- 20Ah battery
- Frame painted satin black
- 34.715mm front fork with thinner wall tubes and polished aluminium legs
- LISPA 320mm rear shock absorbers
- Plastic mudguards and side covers
- Colours red or blue-grey
- Metal fuel tank and side cover badges
- Small fairing with day-glow orange panels
- Instruments inherited from 750 S3 with speedometer and tachometer in rubber sleeves
- No speedometer trip reset
- Tommaselli Daytona 2C throttle (early chrome later black)
- Black handlebar levers
- Single Voxbell horn
- Black-bodied turn signal indicators
- Black lifting handle on the left
- Drilled 300mm and 242mm disc brakes
- Front brake master cylinder with clear reservoir
- Silver-painted FPS cast aluminium wheels

The second series 850 Le Mans was little changed from the first series. This example also has the optional Lafranconi exhaust.

The speedometer now included a trip meter and the tachometer read to 10,000rpm. (Courtesy Two Wheels)

De Tomaso's automotive styling influence was evident in the second series Le Mans taillight.

STYLE WITH SPEED: THE 850 LE MANS (1975-78)

was a plastic cover over the unsightly solenoid. These modifications were accompanied by a new seat and angular taillight, and updated instrument panel. The Veglia speedometer now included a trip reset, and the tachometer read to 10,000rpm with a redline at 8000rpm. The seat was designed to accommodate a passenger more comfortably than before, with a shorter rear hump and holding strap. Still made of slippery plastic-covered foam, it was also more durable than the earlier seat, although there were still complaints regarding premature cracking. The seat attached to a swivelling bracket at the rear.

Accompanying the revised seat was a new rear mudguard and taillight. Displaying De Tomaso's automotive influence, the rear mudguard incorporated a hard-edged, styled oblong taillight. Colour choice expanded to include white. The speedometer and tachometer were encased in a plastic surround but the dashboard warning lights were unchanged. Some of this series also featured black-painted lower fork legs.

> *850 Le Mans distinguishing features second series (from frame number VE 13041-VE 17311)*
>
> Plastic cover over solenoid
> Instruments encased in plastic housing
> Speedometer with trip reset
> New rear mudguard
> New taillight
> Redesigned seat
> White offered alongside red and blue-grey
> Some with black-painted fork legs

A Gazzola-signed factory photo of a second series 850 Le Mans with black fork legs. (Courtesy Ivar de Gier)

73

A 1978 road test photo of the second series 850 Le Mans. The ugly front number plate was required in Australia at that time. (Courtesy Two Wheels)

Wind tunnel design: the Le Mans II & CX 100

During 1977, Lino Tonti resurrected the idle wind tunnel at the factory and began designing a fairing for the next series of touring Moto Guzzi, the 1000 SP. Known as the Spada (sword) in the UK, the 1000 SP was intended by De Tomaso to be Moto Guzzi's V-twin sport touring motorcycle to compete with the BMW R100RS. While BMW used the Pininfarina wind tunnel to develop its R100RS, Tonti was fortunate to have access to a wind tunnel in his back yard. A relic from the 1950s golden racing era, when it was used to design the dustbin fairings for the Grand Prix machines, the wind tunnel had only been used for scientific purposes since 1957. Tonti's only restriction was he had to use the wind tunnel after hours because the electric fan consumed so much power that the production line couldn't operate at the same time!

The resulting 1000 SP fairing was an innovative three-piece design constructed of fibreglass. The top section turned with the handlebars and the two side panels were frame-mounted, incorporating angled aerofoils to increase downthrust at higher speeds. With this new fairing came a redesigned instrument panel in moulded rubber pseudo alligator skin. The 1000 SP went into production in 1978, alongside the Le Mans and was to influence the design of the next sporting Moto Guzzi, the Le Mans II.

The fairing design for the Le Mans II was completed in the wind tunnel at Mandello, which had stood dormant for many years.

Le Mans II (first series; from frame number VE 17312-VE 22635)

The success of the Le Mans proved there was a ready market for a sporting Moto Guzzi V-twin, and during 1978 the Le Mans was updated to incorporate many 1000 SP components. Because this model was officially named the Le Mans II, the earlier Le Mans is often incorrectly called the Le Mans I.

With the Le Mans II, Moto Guzzi followed a path that was often a failing with Italian motorcycle manufacturers. Sometimes, in implementing change for the sake of fashion, a winning formula is unnecessarily altered, which is what happened to the Le Mans in 1978, although other manufacturers such as Ducati also participated in this dubious practice. Functionally, the Le Mans II was similar to the earlier bike, but the 1000 SP-inspired fairing and instruments detracted from the Le Mans' sporting purity and aesthetic appeal. Frame numbers began where the Le Mans finished, at VE 17312, ending at VE 24086, or VE 22635 for the 1978 and 1979 series. As with the Le Mans, this official number series could be incorrect as some Le Mans II were known to have earlier frame numbers.

The engine, gearbox, pistons and silencers carried new part numbers, but there were few changes to the engine and drive train specifications compared to the earlier Le Mans. The VE engine number sequence continued (from around 77000) and, because the big valve, high compression engine was unable to pass new US emission requirements, the Le Mans II wasn't sold there. Moto Guzzi no longer made a horsepower claim for the 844cc motor, now quoting torque of 7.8kgm at 6600rpm.

The alternator cover was black plastic, and there was an oil dipstick extension to enable oil level checking without removal of the fairing. While the black plastic alternator cover didn't look as good as the earlier aluminium type, it was a functional improvement as it included ducting designed to cool the alternator. The alternator was also new for the Le Mans II, although the 14V 20A specification was unchanged. The Dell'Orto PHF36B carburettors were similar, but the gauze for the bell mouths was now aluminium rather than wire (the reason for this was that the wire-type had a tendency to break up and become ingested by the engine).

One improvement was to the gearshift lever mechanism, which incorporated a ball joint at the transmission end of the rod, although the clevis joint was retained at the other end. The black-painted silencers now featured bolt-on foot protector plates. The frame was also unchanged, and carried the same part number.

While the engine, transmission, final drive and frame were similar or identical to those of the earlier Le Mans, the Le Mans II chassis was more akin to that of the 1000 SP. The side stand included two springs, and, as there was a different ignition key location, the plate on the top frame tube was located by a bolt (later bikes with a printed circuit board instrument panel didn't have the plate). The hydraulic steering damper was now longitudinally mounted to the lower triple clamp and frame on the left in order to fit under the new front fairing. Adjustment was now on the steering damper body and was considerably more awkward to effect.

Most of the bodywork was also new for the Le

The new fairing gave the Le Mans II a completely different look.

Mans II. The tank and seat were visually similar to the second series Le Mans, but the tank filler cap was a metal screw cap under a lockable lifting panel. There were also new Paioli petrol taps and a different fuel tank attachment to the frame, which had a plate at the front. The plastic side covers and mudguards were similar to before, the side covers featuring 'LE MANS II' metal badges. The side covers were longer than before, partially covering the carburettor bell mouths. Colours were now red with black, or white with black. Both versions still included day-glow flashes on each side of the headlight.

To accommodate the larger fairing and instrument panel, the front fork assembly was similar to that on the 1000 SP. The 34.715mm fork tubes were thicker than on the earlier Le Mans, with a standard hexagonal spring retaining nut. The dampers were 25mm longer, providing additional fork travel, the amount of fork oil reduced to 0.90 litres per leg. Two separate fork springs had a plastic spacer in-between. The fork width was also increased to 195mm to match that of the 850 T series and SP 1000. Springs were now dual rate

The engine and transmission for the Le Mans II was unchanged, although the gearshift linkage now included a ball joint.

The Le Mans II fuel cap was under a locking flap.

and the lower fork sliders were painted black, with a rear brake caliper mount. There were also new rear 320mm shock absorbers supplied by FUTA, LIMS, or LISPA, depending on the production batch.

The instrument layout, fairing and controls were completely updated for the Le Mans II. The rigidly-mounted fairing lowers were similar to those of the 1000 SP, while the upper fairing was new and turned with the fork. It incorporated the rectangular 45/40 watt headlight, but was smaller than the 1000 SP and included a lower, polycarbonate screen which was smoke-coloured. The front rectangular turn signals were included in the fairing, and there were no rear vision mirrors. The fairing was very angular in shape, typical of the De Tomaso automotive

The Le Mans II instrument panel was much more comprehensive than on earlier versions.

influence, and on most examples wasn't particularly well finished. The upper fairing design was also flawed as the top section could hit the side fairings under full lock. Despite the oil filler extension it was still difficult to check oil level with the fairing lower in place, and the knee cushions were inconveniently sited for taller riders.

Although the fairing was flawed in execution and didn't contribute to the aesthetics of the Le Mans, it was functional as the lower wind tunnel-designed spoilers aided stability. Also similar to that of the SP 1000 was the instrument panel, which incorporated a volt meter and clock that flanked the 10,000rpm tachometer and 240kph speedometer. Instruments were as on the second series 850 Le Mans, and there was a large array of bewildering warning lights underneath in a printed circuit board (some versions included a warning light panel without a printed circuit board). With the updated fairing for the Le Mans II, there was a new wiring loom and rectangular turn signals.

New offset, clip-on handlebars were in black chrome, and there were all-new handlebar switches and controls. The left CEV switch was considerably improved ergonomically, and the black plastic throttle assembly incorporated the starter and ignition stop switches, which necessitated new throttle cables. Also new was the clutch lever assembly and adjuster screw, the wires no longer routed through the handlebars. About the only control feature carried over from the first Le Mans was the handgrips.

Two types of wheel graced the Le Mans II. Most had the same silver-painted FPS as on the previous Le Mans, but a similar Bezzi, with 12 straight spokes, was also fitted and featured in some official publicity material (presumably, the Bezzis were used when FPS stock ran low). Both types of wheels were interchangeable and had 7.5mm flanges between wheel and disc on each side in order to fit the wider fork legs. One improvement was tyre choice: most Le Mans II left the factory with excellent Pirelli Gordon MT 18 tyres, but some still came with old stock Metzelers. The Pirelli tyres provided good dry weather performance, they came under criticism for their wet weather operation; as a result most German and Dutch versions had Metzeler tyres.

The triple disc Brembo integrated braking system was as before, but the front 08 brake calipers were mounted behind the fork legs and included a single bleed valve. Brake pads were as on the Le Mans, but for some markets (such as Germany) the pad type was changed to Ferrit ID 334FG. As with the Le Mans, a full racing uprating kit was available, also as before except that it now included the sump extension originally developed in 1970 for the V7 Sport racers. The sump extension was initially incorporated to aid cooling, but later development allowed a reduction in internal friction as the oil was further from the crankshaft.

When it came to on-the-road performance, the Le Mans II was similar to the Le Mans, despite its additional weight (the claimed dry weight of 196kg was extremely optimistic). The Le Mans II weighed a more realistic 228kg wet. Despite the alleged aerodynamic efficiency of the new fairing, the Le Mans II was no faster than the Le Mans, the Italian magazine *Motociclismo* achieving a top speed of 203.6kph (126.5mph), with a standing 400 metres in 12.198 seconds at 173.127kph (107.6mph).

In most respects the Le Mans II offered little improvement over the Le Mans, and the fit and finish were certainly inferior as De Tomaso sought to cut production costs. Production levels were similar to those of the earlier Le Mans, with 560 manufactured in 1978, 2980 in 1979, and 2786 in 1980. In the UK in 1979 the Le Mans II cost £2477; as this was considerably more than the previous Le Mans, sales were correspondingly modest. The series continued until sometime during 1980.

Le Mans II (second series; from frame number VE 22636-VE 24086)

During 1980 the Le Mans II received some updates, enough to make it a second series. Most engine updates occurred after engine VE 80390, and chassis updates after VE 22636. As engines and frames were always built independently, there was considerable overlap in specification between this and the previous series Le Mans II, although most of these updates were implemented by July 1980.

After engine number 80390 there were new Nigusil-plated cylinders, with matching pistons and new piston rings. First introduced on the smaller V35 and V50, then the 850 T4 in 1979, these cylinders were far superior to the earlier cast-iron and chrome-plated type as they were lighter, ran cooler with tighter tolerances, and provided improved wear characteristics with reduced oil consumption. Nigusil was developed and patented by Moto Guzzi, supposedly different to other hard surface treatments. The process was galvanic, uniformly electrolytically combining solid silicon carbide particles in a nickel deposit.

Some Le Mans II were fitted with 12 spoke wheels, as in this publicity photo. The tyres here are Metzeler. (Courtesy Moto Guzzi)

850 Le Mans II distinguishing features first series (from frame number VE 17312 to VE 22635)

Carburettor bell mouths with aluminium gauze filters
New exhaust silencers with foot protector plates
Black plastic alternator cover
New alternator
Oil dipstick extension
Gearshift mechanism included a new rod and top ball joint
Sidestand included dual springs
Plate on top frame tube bolted in place on bikes without a printed circuit instrument panel
Steering damper longitudinally mounted on the right
Lockable fuel filler flap on tank with revised frame location
Metal fuel tank and side cover badges
New Paioli fuel taps
New mudguards, side covers, and dual seat
Black forward offset handlebars
New CEV switches
Twin pull throttle incorporating start and stop switch
Ignition switch moved to dash panel
Three-piece fairing with fixed side panels
Smoke-coloured screen
Rectangular headlight
Rectangular rear turn signals
New front fork with black lower legs and 195mm fork width
New 320mm rear shock absorbers
Some examples with Bezzi cast aluminium wheels with straight spokes
Front wheel included 7.5mm flanges between wheel and disc
Front Brembo calipers mounted behind fork legs
Pirelli Gordon MT18 tyres generally fitted

Front view of the Le Mans II. The fork legs were more widely spaced than on earlier Le Mans. (Courtesy Moto Guzzi)

Several other engine updates occurred during 1980, but these were not necessarily restricted to engines after number 80390. These updates comprised new cylinder heads, a new crankshaft, new connecting rods, and new lower pushrod plungers. At the same time there was a new rear cover for the transmission, interchangeable with the earlier version.

As the larger, 32 Ah battery was standardized around this time, there was a new battery tray. Also updated were the lower frame rails, and there was a new side stand and new footpeg arms. Bodywork updates included replacement plastic side covers, plus a new front brake lever. From frame number

WIND TUNNEL DESIGN: THE LE MANS II & CX 100

VE 22636 air-adjustable LISPA dampers were incorporated with individual valves for each fork leg, whilst at the rear were new, air-assisted Paioli shock absorbers with lighter springs. Accompanying the new suspension was a stronger centre stand with a longer tang. First seen on the 1000 SP, this was to obviate premature breakage of the centre stand (a problem on the earlier Le Mans II), and also help with getting the bike on the stand. Tyre choice expanded to include excellent Pirelli Phantoms (MT29 and MT28).

Although about to be replaced by the new generation Le Mans III in 1981, 1009 Le Mans IIs were constructed in 1980, and many of these sat unsold in distributor warehouses. Some were repainted as the Le Mans Black and Gold by British importer, Coburn and Hughes, for the British market, a significant cosmetic alteration along the lines of the Ducati 900 Super Sport which was introduced at the same time. The bodywork was painted black, with gold 750 S-style flashes, and the wheels and lower fork legs painted gold. The price rose to £2999.

The CX 100 1979

As the high compression, big valve, 850cc engine couldn't satisfy new US emission standards imposed on motorcycles manufactured after January 1 1978, a specific Le Mans was created for the US for 1979. American buyers also required larger displacement engines, and the importer, Berliner, asked for a 1000cc Le Mans. This hybrid model, the CX 100, was essentially a touring 1000cc SP engine in a Le Mans II chassis. The CX 100 didn't have the same performance as the Le Mans, but the power was usable and it was a surprisingly successful amalgam of two models.

Engine numbers for the CX 100 were shared with the 1000 SP series, beginning around VG 206500. Introduced in 1978, the 1000 SP engine displaced 948.8cc, and with the normal 78mm

Most Le Mans II were fitted with FPS wheels and Pirelli Gordon tyres, as on this example. (Courtesy Moto Guzzi)

> *850 Le Mans II distinguishing features second series (from July 1980 frame number VE 22636-VE 24086; from engine number VE 80390)*
>
> *Nigusil cylinders and matching pistons (from engine 80390)*
> *New cylinder heads*
> *New crankshaft*
> *New con-rod assembly*
> *New pushrod valve plungers*
> *New rear cover for transmission*
> *New battery plate for larger battery*
> *New lower frame rails*
> *New side stand*
> *New footpeg arms*
> *New side covers*
> *New front brake lever*
> *Air assisted front fork (from frame 22636)*
> *Air-assisted rear Paioli shock absorbers*
> *Stronger centre stand with longer tang*
> *Tyres included Pirelli Phantom MT29 and MT28*

assemblies). While other Italian motorcycles with Dell'Orto carburettors had their air screws locked in place to comply with new EPA requirements, CX 100 air screws were adjustable. Compared with European 1000s, the US carburettors came with a leaner throttle slide and different idle mixture screw. Although the parts catalogue describes the cables as those of the Le Mans II, the CX 100 required shorter pull cables for the smaller carburettors. Unlike the Le Mans II, the carburettors breathed through a 1000 SP airbox with a circular pleated paper air filter.

The engine breather system was different to that of the Le Mans and Le Mans II as the breather was combined with the airbox. Instead of the earlier, stroke the flat-topped, three-ring, 88mm pistons provided a lower compression ratio of 9.2:1. The combustion chamber contained smaller valves (41mm intake and 36mm exhaust), and measured 72mm in diameter with a depth of 26mm. Cylinder liners were cast-iron, and the camshaft the same as on the Le Mans and Le Mans II. The CX 100 also included the lighter Le Mans flywheel, along with primary drive, transmission, and final drive.

The lower end was the same as on the 1000 SP, with connecting rods now including oil passages from the big-end bearing to both sides of the piston in the small end; on the Le Mans and Le Mans II, the oil passage was to the thrust side only. The ignition distributor was the 1000 SP Marelli S311B, providing a fixed advance of 2 degrees and full advance of 33 degrees. The intake and exhaust system also came from the 1000 SP, and carburation was by Dell'Orto VHB 30C (square-slide) carburettors with accelerator pumps (the same type as used on the earlier V7 Sport, with accelerator pumps incorporated in the needle jet

This black and gold 850 Le Mans II was available in the UK market during 1981.

Although available in limited numbers only, the black and gold Le Mans II was nevertheless widely advertised in the motorcycle press. (Courtesy Ivar de Gier)

one-way flapper valve there was a one-way check ball valve inside the hose connecting the engine breather to the airbox. The ball was retained by a steel plate and could stick if the engine wasn't used regularly. The exhaust system also came from the 1000 SP – painted black instead of chrome-plated – and included only a single balance tube under the transmission. Moto Guzzi made no horsepower claim for the CX 100, and whilst this was certainly less than that of the 850 Le Mans, torque was up to 8.6kgm at 5200rpm.

The CX 100 chassis was very similar to that of the Le Mans II, but carried a new frame number sequence beginning at VU 111111, continuing until VU 111383 for the 1979 series. Specification differences to the Le Mans II included a sealed beam Wagner 60/40 watt headlight with associated brackets, speedometer reading to 160mph (or the later mandatory 80mph), and 'CX 100' badges on the side covers. Other details included front and rear round reflectors and the 20 Ah Le Mans battery. Colours were either red or white.

With only 281 CX 100s manufactured in 1979, this was a rare model. Compared to the earlier Le Mans the CX 100 was heavier and slower. *Cycle* magazine, in the July 1980 issue, recorded a weight of 240.4kg (530lb) wet for its machine, commenting that: "Like many automobiles and motorcycles – and people – the Le Mans has gained weight in advancing years." The test bike performed only slightly slower than the 1977 Le Mans, however, with the standing quarter mile covered in 13.50 seconds at 98.46mph (158kph).

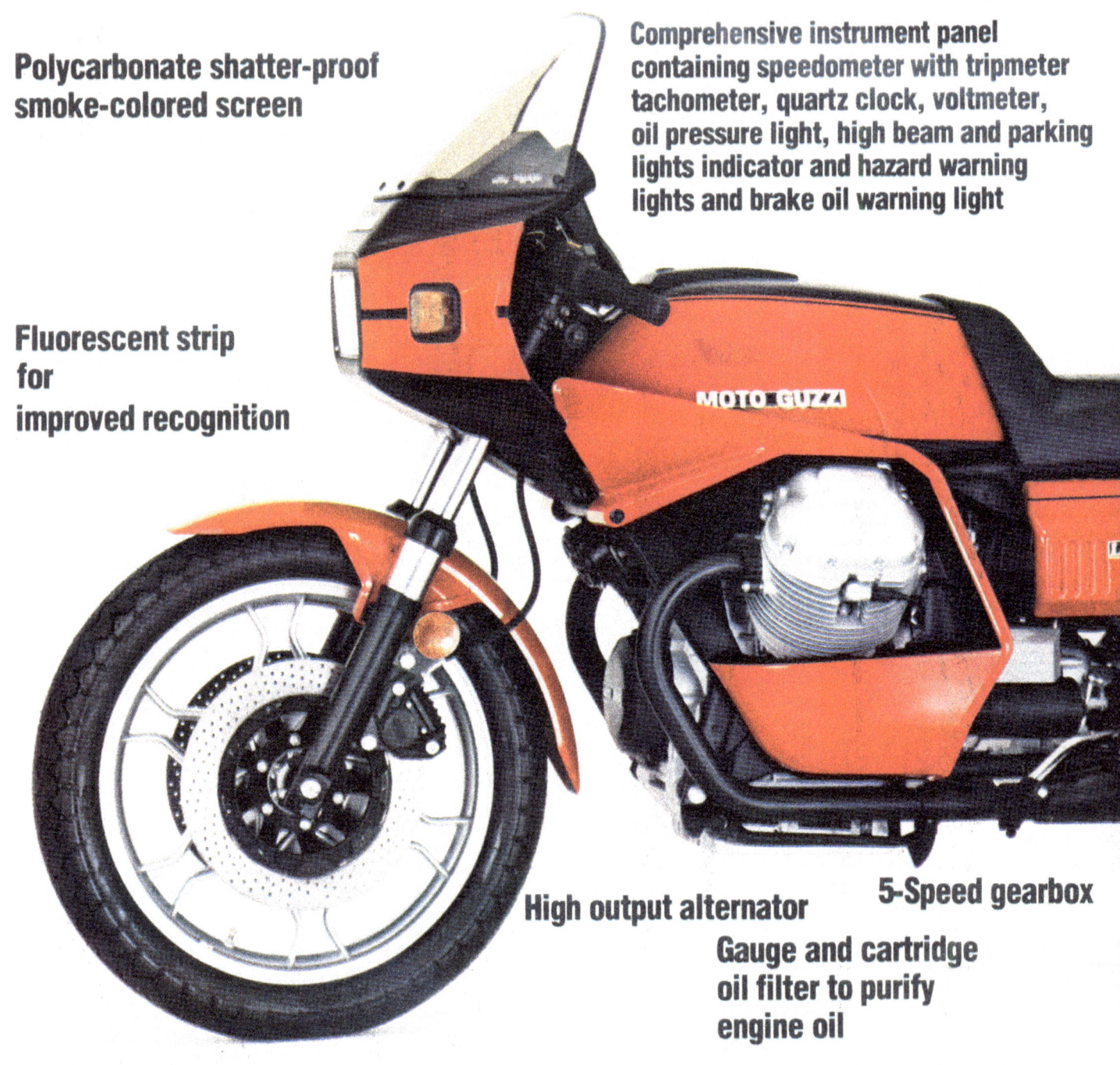

A Masterpiece Of Elegance And Craftsmanship

Polycarbonate shatter-proof smoke-colored screen

Comprehensive instrument panel containing speedometer with tripmeter tachometer, quartz clock, voltmeter, oil pressure light, high beam and parking lights indicator and hazard warning lights and brake oil warning light

Fluorescent strip for improved recognition

High output alternator

5-Speed gearbox

Gauge and cartridge oil filter to purify engine oil

Twin front and single rear discs made from cast iron and drilled to improve thermal efficiency and water dispersal

WIND TUNNEL DESIGN: THE LE MANS II & CX 100

CX 100 1981

At a 1979 price of $4949, the CX 100 wasn't a resounding success in America, and none was produced for 1980. Prior to the release of the Le Mans III, however, a small batch – just **72** – of updated CX 100s was built in 1981, and incorporated many of the Le Mans II and 1000 SP updates. The engines were still 1000 SP, and from engine number VG 215000 featured Nigusil cylinders and matching pistons, and most had Dell'Orto PHF 30 carburettors mounted on rubber intakes. The round slide carburettors had special lean burn jetting to comply with US emissions regulations (also a feature of the US 1000 SP and G-5 of the same era).

Frame numbers carried on from VU 111384, finishing at around VU 111460. Most of the chassis of this final series of CX 100s incorporated the air-adjustable LISPA dampers with individual valves for each fork leg, and the air-assisted Paioli shock absorbers with lighter springs that featured on the second series Le Mans II.

At this stage Moto Guzzis were still distributed by the Premier Motor Corporation in America, and the CX 100 was listed until 1982, by which time the price had risen to $5498. Only 353 CX 100s were produced in total; it remains a unique model in the history of the sporting Moto Guzzi.

Light alloy cast wheels

Hasbrouck Heights, N.J. 07604
45 years of motorcycle experience and
and a constant flow of genuine spare parts.

CX 100 distinguishing features (from frame number VU 111111)

949cc engine with 9.2:1 88mm three-ring pistons
Nigusil cylinders and matching pistons from engine 215000
Smaller (41mm and 36mm) valves
Dell'Orto VHB 30 C carburettors with air filter
Dell'Orto PHF 30 carburettors on rubber manifolds for second series
Black-painted exhaust system without front balance tube
Air-assisted suspension for second series
Sealed beam headlight
'CX 100' side cover badges
Round front and rear reflectors
160 or 80 mph speedometer
20Ah battery

For the US the Le Mans II was only available as the CX 100, with the 1000cc engine of the SP 1000.

6 square heads

By the end of the 1970s Moto Guzzi found itself at a crossroad with the large capacity twins. De Tomaso was determined to both expand production and reduce costs, and during the early and mid-1970s Tonti spent much of his time and energy developing the new range of smaller capacity V twins. As the Mandello plant couldn't cope with a massive increase in production, by 1979, small twin engine production had moved to the old Innocenti factory in Milan, purchased by De Tomaso in 1975. Unfortunately, the small twins proved expensive to produce, and also suffered from poor quality control, plus the necessary intensive development restricted the updates that could be made to the big twins, in particular the sporting Le Mans. Apart from the new fairing introduced on the Le Mans II, this series soldiered on through until 1980 with minimal development.

While the small twins were initially conventionally styled, in 1979 Moto Guzzi released two sporting versions: the V35 Imola and V50 Monza. Their new, angular fairing and tailpiece shapes were designed by De Tomaso's automotive division at Modena, and were one of the few examples of successful integration of automotive styling on a motorcycle. The styling of the smaller sporting Guzzi twins met with acclaim and would influence the next generation Le Mans.

Le Mans III

Although a significant number of Le Mans II were manufactured, the big valve, 844cc engine was having trouble complying with tougher noise and emission regulations. Already unable to pass US tests, the days of open bell mouth carburettors were also numbered for Europe and the rest of the world.

To maintain existing performance levels the large capacity, air-cooled twin would need a more efficient intake and exhaust system, which is what Moto Guzzi did to the Le Mans, in the process, restyling and updating it for the 1980s. While the Le Mans II was an efficient design, it lacked the styling purity of the original Le Mans, and some appeal as a minimalist sporting motorcycle, made evident in recent years as owners have converted Le Mans II back to Le Mans specification. Moto Guzzi lost some sporting direction with the Le Mans II, but made up for it with the new Le Mans III. The Le Mans III appeared to be a simple restyle, but there was more to the new design than angular styling and square cylinders and heads. The 44 official updates between the Le Mans III and Le Mans II – although many were minor improvements – meant it was effectively a new motorcycle.

Engine and transmission

Engine numbers began at VF 011111 but while the shape of the cylinders and heads was new, internally there were few changes. Capacity remained at 844cc, valve sizes at 44 and 37mm, and valve length 106mm (inlet) and 105mm (exhaust). The combustion chamber was also unchanged at 74mm in diameter with a depth of 27mm.

Rocker breathers were now a screw fitting instead of crimped, and the rocker oil feeds internal. The cylinders were Nigusil-plated as they were on the second series Le Mans II, with matching pistons as before. A thicker cylinder head gasket slightly

Although the cylinder head design for the Le Mans III stayed the same, the rocker oil feed was now internal.

lowered compression ratio to 9.8:1. The camshaft and distributor were the same, but there were new Dell'Orto PHF BD and BS carburettors, still with diaphragm accelerator pumps. While retaining the rubber manifolds, these were re-jetted for a new airbox and exhaust system. US examples (when the model finally reached the US in 1983) included even leaner jetting; a 115 main jet instead of 132 and a 50 idle jet instead of 60. To answer criticism of excessively strong carburettor springs, there were new versions; longer (134v130mm), with fewer windings (15v18) and a slightly thicker gauge wire, but there was very little difference in throttle action and it remained heavy. The choke lever was relocated underneath the carburettor on the left.

Inside the engine was a heavier crankshaft,

The 850 Le Mans III was more than a style update, incorporating, as it did, 44 technical modifications.

The intake and exhaust system was completely new, and allowed the Le Mans III to comply with new noise and emission controls. The square cylinders and heads gave a new look.

statically balanced by adding 1.650-1.652kg of weight instead of 1.586-1.616kg to smooth out running at low speed. There were new autolube con-rod bearings along with con-rods slightly thinner at the base (23.8mm instead of 23.98mm). Aluminium, instead of cast-iron, rocker supports now expanded at the same rate as the cylinder heads, allowing closer operating tolerances and reducing valve train noise. Unfortunately, the alloy rocker supports didn't absorb the sound as efficiently as the more solid cast-iron versions, somewhat negating the noise reduction benefit. Apart from wider cylinder stud spacing there were no changes to the crankcases, which continued to feature external webbing. The wider cylinder studs made it easy for Moto Guzzi to build the next generation 949cc Le Mans as it readily accepted the 88mm Nigusil cylinders from the SP 1000. The aluminium sump spacer of the late Le Mans II racing uprating kit was also included. The dry clutch was unchanged with Ferodo type I/F324 clutch plates.

It took a lot of development to enable the 844cc, twin cylinder engine to pass new CEE 78.1015 European noise and emission controls, and still produce acceptable power. But Guzzi's engineers, headed by the legendary Umberto Todero, managed to create an airbox and exhaust system that was quieter than the Le Mans and Le Mans II, but produced more power. The air filter was a more efficient flat rectangular type inside an airbox with a long snorkel between the carburettors. The chrome-plated exhaust system featured double-walled exhaust header pipes and much larger mufflers. These mufflers were quieter, producing a deeper exhaust note, and the dual-walled header pipes resisted blueing more effectively than the earlier V7 Sport and 750 S. As on the CX 100 there was no crossover pipe in front of the engine, but the crossover underneath the gearbox remained. The new crankcase and cylinder head ventilation system used the frame backbone as a chamber, before venting to the atmosphere through the airbox. The air venting tube was placed higher up the frame than the oil return tube. The same one-way check ball as on the CX 100 was used in the breather outlet tube. Condensed oil return to the crankcase was by a rubber tube from the rear frame cross tube to the oil return on the crankcase. In addition to the modified engine breathing arrangement, the transmission breather was also moved from the left front to the rear cover; an improvement as there was less oil frothing at the rear of the transmission, and the problem of oil leakage on earlier transmissions was largely overcome.

Although official documentation didn't state a horsepower figure for the Le Mans III, the factory did claim increased power (by 3hp) compared to the Le Mans II and Le Mans. A racing uprating kit was still available for the Le Mans III, including the B10 camshaft, Dell'Orto PHM 40 B carburettors and manifolds, racing exhaust system, and the straight cut, close ratio gearbox.

Chassis

The Le Mans III carried a new set of frame numbers, beginning at VF 11111 and running through to VF 20700. Apart from the crankcase ventilation chamber incorporated in the frame backbone tube, the Tonti-designed frame was much as before. The steering lock remained the Neiman on the steering head, and a hydraulic steering damper was located on the right with a manual adjuster (as on the Le Mans II).

To increase the wheelbase, providing improved high speed stability and more passenger room, the swingarm was lengthened to 410mm. The wheelbase increased to 1505mm and required a longer transmission shaft. There was no change in the swingarm width, and the Le Mans III was still restricted to a narrow section rear tyre. This wasn't really a functional problem as wider tyres were more a fashion accessory than a necessity on the Tonti-frame Moto Guzzi. Lino Tonti once told Ivar de Gier that the easiest way to improve the handling of any Tonti-frame Moto Guzzi big twin was to fit the wheels and tyre size of the original V7 Sport. Ivar tried this on his California III. "It looked strange, those skinny tyres on the large California, but the handling and steering were greatly improved, and I was sold on the idea," says Ivar.

The 850 Le Mans III included air-assistance for the front fork; the two legs were linked.

The Paioli rear shock absorbers were also air-assisted.

were also new, and slightly longer than those of the Le Mans II at 330mm. Travel was 75mm and the chrome-plated springs were mounted upside down with spring preload at the top. The right shock absorber included an air pressure valve, linked to the left by a plastic tube; required air pressure was 3-5kg/sq cm (42-70psi).

In 1983 the Paioli shock absorbers acquired fins on the body near the air valve but were still mounted upside down. The quality of the Paioli shock absorbers was very poor, and, as with the fork, air pressure was extremely difficult to set up. The plastic connecting tubes were also prone to breakage.

The silver-painted FPS wheels were as before

All 850 Le Mans IIIs featured DayGlo flashes on the fairing, but the metallic grey seen here was less common. (Courtesy Moto Guzzi)

There was also new suspension for the Le Mans III, and while Moto Guzzi still used a front fork with skinny, 34.715mm tubes, the fork was longer (407.5mm), and provided more travel (148.5mm). As on the final Le Mans II, the forks were air-assisted, but both tubes were now linked. The valve was on the top of the right fork tube and air pressure was a very modest 2-3kg/sq cm (28-42psi). Air-assisted suspension was fashionable in the early 1980s but was difficult to set accurately as the air chamber was extremely small and required a supplementary gasket in the pressure gauge head. The lower fork legs were painted the same colour as the bodywork, and fork width was the same 180mm of the V7 Sport and first Le Mans. The rear Paioli shock absorbers

but with a new front wheel hub and without the Le Mans II 7.5mm spacers. As on the Le Mans II, two types of wheel were described in the parts catalogue although most Le Mans III were fitted with FPS. Tyre sizes remained a narrow Pirelli Phantom MT29 and MT28 (100/90V18 and 110/90V18). As on the earlier Le Mans it was not possible to fit a larger rear tyre as this would foul the taillight and rear indicator wires; this wasn't a functional problem, however, as larger tyres on the Le Mans were more a fashion consideration than anything else.

The integrated brakes were also unchanged from the Le Mans II, retaining the 12mm round reservoir front master cylinder with a clear reservoir, and drilled 300mm and 242mm cast-iron discs. German market Le Mans III included different brake pads (non-asbestos Ferrit ID 334), and also a larger Brembo F09 rear brake caliper (with 48mm rather than 38mm pistons). This larger rear brake caliper gave improved braking and was combined with a proportioning valve instead of a four-way manifold. The caliper and proportioning valve came from the 1000 SP and transferred increased braking pressure to the front wheel as more brake was applied. It was surprising that this improved braking set-up was only used on the German models.

Most changes were cosmetic, including a reshaped, 25 litre fuel tank, new side covers with metal '850 Le Mans III' badges, and a smaller wind tunnel-designed fairing similar to the Le Mans II

One of the Le Mans III's most individual touches was the dashboard, with its large, centrally located, white-faced tachometer. The handlebar switches were also new.

version in that it had a handlebar-mounted top section and frame-mounted side panels, but of a new shape with smaller side panels which no longer encompassed the engine. Missing was an extension for the dipstick as the lower section of the engine was now exposed as on the first Le Mans, the result of which was a much more sporting appearance. The upper fairing still incorporated the 45/40 watt rectangular headlight and turn signals, but these were no longer integrated flush with the fairing. Instead of badges, the tank and fairing had decals of a gold eagle, with black outline on the tank. Three new colours were offered for the Le Mans III (red, white, and metallic grey), and each included black and day-glow flashes on the front of the fairing.

Although the fairing shape was new, the instrument panel represented the biggest departure in cockpit design compared with the earlier Le Mans II. Dominated by a large (100mm), white-faced, Veglia tachometer, and flanked by a voltmeter and 240kh speedometer, the instrument layout was fashionable and effective. US versions initially had an 80mph speedometer. The six warning light panel was also more up-to-date, and this asymmetrical and unusual instrument layout probably sold Moto Guzzi a large number of Le Mans III. Accompanying the instrument console was another set of new handlebar switches, although the forward offset clip-on handlebars went unchanged. There was also a new black plastic throttle and engine stop switch. The seat was redesigned: hard and narrow and not particularly comfortable. A neat touch was the spring clip which retained the strap that had to be removed in order to lift the seat to access the tool tray.

To compensate for the longer suspension, footpeg position was moved to 75mm below and in front of the swingarm pivot, and fixed with new, grid-type milled brackets. The battery was upgraded to 24 Ah but, in many respects, the Le Mans III was still a relic of the 1970s as, in 1981, few motorcycles remained still with battery and points ignition, plus the skinny, 35mm front fork was underwhelming, and most large capacity sporting motorcycles were also fitted with wider rims and larger tyres.

But when it came to style and usable, all-round performance, the Le Mans III was very much at the forefront. The smaller fairing meant a slight reduction in claimed weight to 206kg, and new intake and exhaust system provided improved engine performance. *Motociclismo* magazine, testing engine number VF 011755 in November

SQUARE HEADS

White was also a colour option. (Courtesy Moto Guzzi)

Only a few 1980s motorcycles presented such a narrow profile. (Courtesy Moto Guzzi)

The rear profile of the Le Mans III, with its narrow tyre, was still reminiscent of an earlier era. (Courtesy Moto Guzzi)

Lean and narrow, the 850 Le Mans III was a superb sporting motorcycle. (Courtesy Two Wheels)

1981, achieved a top speed of 210.120kph (130mph), and a standing 400 metre time of 11.950 seconds at 175.600kphh (109mph). This was still some way off Moto Guzzi's claimed top speed of 230kph, but was impressive all the same. When the Le Mans III finally arrived in the US in 1983, *Cycle* magazine borrowed one, and in September that year found it faster and quieter than the original Le Mans it had tested in 1977. Standing start quarter mile was reached in 12.66 seconds at a speed of 106.38mph (171kph), despite a wet weight of 240.9kg

In the UK the Le Mans III was still distributed by Coburn & Hughes of Luton, retailing at £2899 in 1982, and rising to £3199 in 1983. US Moto Guzzi distribution changed in 1982, delaying the introduction of the Le Mans III. De Tomaso wanted to consolidate distribution in North America, creating Benelli North America as part of his Maserati automobile distribution. Headed by George A Garbutt, but still controlled directly by De Tomaso, Benelli NA introduced a more competitive pricing structure. When it was released in the US during 1983, the Le Mans III was considerably cheaper than the previous CX 100 at $4518.

SQUARE HEADS

Le Mans III production began at the end of 1980 and continued until 1985. Well developed and epitomising the finest aspects of the Le Mans line, with over 10,000 produced, the Le Mans III was the most successful of all the sporting Moto Guzzis. It

The 850 Le Mans III mufflers were quieter and more efficient than on earlier Le Mans models.

was an attractive machine, retaining the compact dimensions of its predecessor, and capable of performance on a par with other 850 and 900cc motorcycles. The Le Mans III was the perfect machine for riders who appreciated the virtues and simplicity of older motorcycles, but who required modern levels of performance and civility.

850 Le Mans III distinguishing features (from frame number VF 11111-VF 20700)

Square-shaped cylinder heads
Internal rocker oil feeds
Screw fitting for rocker breathers
Nigusil cylinders and pistons
Thicker cylinder head gaskets
Heavier crankshaft
Con-rods with a thinner base
Autolube con-rod bearings
Aluminium sump spacer
New sump gasket
No dipstick extension
New Dell'Orto PHF 36B carburettors
Redesigned air filter and airbox
Crankcase and cylinder head fumes vented
  through the frame top tube
Transmission breather moved to the rear cover
Longer transmission driveshaft
New fuel lines

New throttle assembly with revised engine stop
  switch
New carburettor springs
Completely new exhaust system with
  double-walled headers and larger mufflers
New footpeg and silencer brackets
New frame incorporating engine breather in top
  frame tube
New front fork (407.5mm) 180mm spacing and
  red fork tubes
Air-assisted 330mm Paioli shock absorbers with
  new springs
New plate and clip for the steering damper
New front wheel hub
Larger fuel tank with new decals
New side covers and badges
New pedals
New seat padding
New seat support
New mudguards
New turn signal indicators
New headlight and taillight
New dashboard, instruments and cables
24Ah battery
New starter motor support

The 850 Le Mans III was another classic sporting Moto Guzzi.

7

End of the line: Le Mans 1000

As the Moto Guzzi V-twin had existed in 949cc form since the ill-fated Convert of 1975, a 1000cc Le Mans was always expected. It was surprising that it took so long to appear, especially as the 850 Le Mans III engine was already designed to accept the larger 88mm cylinders it would require.

Some well publicised Le Mans 1000s had already been created by distributors around the world, including Peter Stevens in Australia and Motobecane in Germany. The German version appeared in 1982 and incorporated Dell'Orto PHM 40mm carburettors, boasted 85 horsepower, and was resplendent in full fairing. But the delay in implementing production was a traditional Moto Guzzi characteristic.

The groundwork for the first Le Mans was done five years before the eventual production version appeared, and even the V7 Sport took more than a year to come to fruition due to industrial problems. This situation wasn't confined to Moto Guzzi, as both Laverda and Ducati also took longer than expected to implement production of already announced models during the 1980s.

When it appeared at the end of 1984, the Le Mans 1000 showed signs of a hasty conception, and was initially a disappointing endorsement of fashionable trends. De Tomaso was always a strong follower of fashion, and nothing epitomised this more than the Le Mans 1000. De Tomaso personally advocated the 16 inch front wheel and swooping, Lario-inspired styling, as a result of which the Le Mans 1000 should have been superior to the Le Mans III, but was, initially, a lesser motorcycle. The mid-eighties obsession with "bigger is better" wasn't only confined to Moto Guzzi, although the first 1000cc Le Mans was one of the worst examples of this dubious philosophy.

Production also coincided with a period when overall quality and assembly standards were very mediocre, and the Le Mans 1000 acquired a

While it continued the Le Mans tradition in some respects, the 1984 Le Mans 1000 had styling similar to that of the 650 Lario. (Courtesy Moto Guzzi)

poor reputation. Although Moto Guzzi did much to improve the Le Mans 1000 over its ten year lifespan, most of the damage was done in the early years and demand and production was modest with only 6343 examples produced between 1984 and 1993.

Le Mans 1000 first series 1984-85 (from frame number VV 11111)

Often called the Le Mans IV, in factory data this model is known only as the Le Mans 1000. Although frame numbers began with a new VV series, many examples (particularly US ones) now included a 17 digit VIN on the steering head. The VIN consisted of Z (Italy) GU (Guzzi) VV (Le Mans 1000), four digits determined by a particular country code, a year code (A-H from 1980), M (for Mandello) and six digits from 100001. With factory data listing some modifications by frame number and others by VIN, it can be difficult to determine exactly when updates occurred.

By the early 1980s a Le Mans 1000 had become inevitable. Motorcycles were becoming more

Inside the Le Mans 1000 engine was a B10 camshaft and larger valves, providing better performance than the 850. Rocker covers were black in 1984. (Courtesy Two Wheels)

END OF THE LINE: LE MANS 1000

powerful, and the only way to maintain existing performance levels in the wake of increased noise legislation was via increased engine capacity. Fashion trends of 1984 also dictated a 16 inch front wheel, and this is where Moto Guzzi failed. While other manufacturers were designing their chassis around the smaller wheel, Moto Guzzi attached the 16 incher to the existing Tonti frame designed for 18 inch wheels front and rear. It was a questionable decision, and unfortunate for Moto Guzzi as 16 inch wheels were a shortlived answer to the search for quicker steering.

A further shortcoming of the Le Mans 1000 – compared to the earlier 850 – was an overall increase in size and weight, particularly evident when the Le Mans 1000 was sitting alongside a V7 Sport or early Le Mans. So much larger was the Le Mans 1000, in fact, that this seemed a backward step, even though other Italian manufacturers were also producing updates of motorcycles originally designed in the early 1970s. In 1984, Ducati and Laverda were building 1000cc motorcycles which offered little functional improvement over the decade older originals!

Engine and transmission

With a new VV prefix, the 949cc engine of the 1000 Le Mans was considerably uprated, compared with those of the earlier CX 100 and 850 Le Mans III, and the most powerful Moto Guzzi twin yet. Both the valves and combustion chamber were enlarged further, requiring very high domed, three-ring pistons to achieve an acceptably high compression ratio of 10:1 with the large combustion chamber. Valve sizes were now 47mm for the inlet, and 40mm for the exhaust, and stems remained 8mm.

There were also new double valve springs; a 56mm outer and 45mm inner. The larger combustion chamber was 82mm wide with a depth of 30.5mm, requiring shorter (49mm) valve guides. There was very little room for an effective squish band, and this engine still had difficulty complying with emission requirements in some countries.

To further boost performance the Le Mans 1000 received a new camshaft, the same B10 version previously available in the earlier Le Mans racing kit. Providing more valve lift (7.2mm) for both inlet and exhaust valves, valve timing was more sporting than even the earlier V7 Sport camshaft. The inlet valve opened 29 degrees before top dead centre, closing 60 degrees after bottom dead centre, and the exhaust valve opened 58 degrees before bottom dead centre, closing 31 degrees after top dead centre. The crankshaft and con-rods were similar to those of the 850 Le Mans III, with the static crankshaft balance unchanged at 1.650kg. The flywheel was the same as that used on the previous Le Mans 850, and the ignition system the same dual point Marelli with coils and centrifugal advance that first appeared on the V7 Sport. The sparkplug caps were Bosch, with a 5000ohm resistance to suppress ignition interference (the resistance was particularly important for the correct operation of the turn signals).

Completing the performance package was a set of Dell'Orto PHM 40N carburettors, with some of the strongest throttle return springs available at the time, mounted on large diameter rubber manifolds. The Dell'Orto bodies and float bowl were grey, not

Dell'Orto PHM 40A carburettors fed the larger Le Mans 1000 cylinders. These still included extremely strong throttle valve return springs, plus an awkward choke arrangement.

aluminium, in colour. The carburettor to manifold clamps were black-painted steel (instead of stainless steel), with an improved tightening system, and the float bowl retaining nut went up to 22mm (from 14mm). The carburettor chokes included a cable passing through a right-angle connection to an awkward black plastic lever underneath the intake manifold. To meet US emission standards Moto Guzzi fitted a richer slide (50/3), different needle (K33), and leaner needle jet (260). The airbox with flat filter and snorkel intake was similar to the 850 le Mans III. Along with the black plastic alternator cover were black valve covers, the rocker breathers also incorporating a screw fitting and internal oil passages, as on the 850 Le Mans III.

The engine breather set-up was also updated for the Le Mans 1000. Whilst retaining the frame backbone tube as a condensing chamber, oil now returned to the engine via vents in the valve covers, rather than the single return tube to the crankcase parallel to the breather tube. There was an improved check ball valve, retained by a circlip, and the small metal oil return tube near the breather outlet was deleted. The transmission breather remained on the rear cover as on the Le Mans III, and the gearshift return spring was updated, constructed of slightly thinner (3mm) wire to reduce shifting effort. There was also a new gearshift detent mechanism.

Although the primary drive and transmission were unchanged from the Le Mans III, there was a new clutch plate design for the Le Mans 1000, which had a steel core plate between the two riveted friction surfaces. Although this new plate resolved the earlier problem of a sticky clutch in low throttle use, the transmission input spline still suffered from premature wear, another problem that Moto Guzzi refused to address for some unknown reason. The Bosch electric start was the same 0.7 Kw version as before, but the solenoid plastic cover was often left off during assembly at the factory. The solenoid was still above the starter motor which was stretched to the limit in starting the high compression big twin, especially with a standard 24Ah battery.

Also new was the black, chrome-plated exhaust system, the exhaust header pipes retained by full circle collars instead of the previous split type. The exhaust system now included a large sheet metal crossover under the transmission instead of the earlier tubular steel type. This crossover was hollow on the Le Mans 1000 and the size such that it had to be removed to drain the transmission oil. The result of these engine developments saw torque increase to 8.43kgm at 6300rpm, and power to a healthy (if not groundbreaking) 81hp at 7000rpm.

The Le Mans 1000 engine exemplified the result of nearly 15 years of evolution, and in many respects was the finest of the sporting Moto Guzzi motors. Although not as smooth as the smaller capacity examples, power delivery was superior. By 1993, it had been further improved, but always retained a strong link with earlier versions. The idiosyncrasies of dual points ignition and oil filter in the sump would remain with the Le Mans until the end.

Chassis

As previously mentioned, frame numbers began at VV 11111 but many examples had a 17 digit VIN. While the black-painted frame was still the Tonti design of the first V7 Sport, it was now the updated type first introduced on the second series 850 T5 of 1984, and included a longer steering head (212mm instead of 165mm), and additional gusset connecting the top of the steering head to the top frame tube (as on the California II). The rear subframe also bent upward to accommodate the new-style seat and tail.

Although the frame was painted black on the early Le Mans 1000, it had red-painted, removable lower rails to match the wheels, plus a new swingarm which, although the same length as that of the 850 Le Mans III, was wider to accommodate the larger section rear tyre. The left swingarm fork was bowed outward to provide a width of 130mm (instead of 115mm). Although the swingarm was the same length as before, with the new frame the wheelbase increased to a substantial 1514mm (59.6 inches). As the mid-1980s trend in sports motorcycles was toward a shorter wheelbase, the Le Mans 1000 moved further outside the mainstream. Steering geometry was also different, with a 28 degree steering head angle and only 98mm of trail. The centre stand retained a long tang, and there was a new side stand, located further back because of the belly pan underneath the motor.

One modification that was an improvement over earlier versions was the introduction of a stouter front fork. Even on the V7 Sport the 35mm fork was marginal, and this was particularly unsatisfactory by 1984. The front fork tubes increased in diameter to a much more appropriate 40mm (39.96mm measured), but retained the internal sealed Paioli dampers. These were 446mm long, and inside each fork leg were dual springs, a 236.5mm upper spring and 229.5mm lower spring, still with air-assistance (1.5-2.5kg/cm^2). During 1985, the Paioli dampers were replaced by Sebac examples, and featured a different connecting hose. As with the Le Mans and Le Mans III, the aluminium triple clamps placed the fork tubes 180mm apart. The fork also included an integral brace, and the stroke was increased to 140mm. The larger fork also required more fluid – 150cc of ATF Dexron – and the fork legs were painted either red or white to match the bodywork.

Despite its flaws, the 1984 Le Mans 1000 was an attractive-looking motorcycle. (Courtesy Two Wheels)

Moto Guzzi Sport & Le Mans Bible

Standard on the Le Mans 1000 was one of the best shock absorbers available; the Koni P7610.

Completing the updated suspension was a pair of 337mm, Koni 'Dial-a-Ride' P7610 shock absorbers with a stroke of 68mm. Although twin shock absorber rear suspension systems were considered outdated, the Koni shock absorbers were amongst the best available and provided excellent rear suspension action; the downside was their increased length which raised seat height and centre of gravity, contributing to the top-heavy and ponderous feel the Le Mans 1000 had compared with earlier versions.

When it came to wheel size Moto Guzzi, unfortunately, followed fashionable trends and fitted a wide, 16 inch front wheel. The cast wheel was a new design, with a five-by-two spoke pattern, the inner rim painted red. While the front wheel boasted a wider MT2.50 inch rim width and was suitable for a tubeless, 120/80V16 inch tyre, the 16 inch wheel did little to enhance the steering or stability of the Le Mans 1000. It appeared that Moto Guzzi had simply decided to climb on the bandwagon by introducing a 16 inch front wheel without testing it sufficiently. The rear wheel remained an 18 inch, although rim width was increased to MT3.00 inch to allow for a larger, 130/80V18 tubeless tyre. Most tyres were very hard compound Michelin A48 and M48. Michelin seemed to have a monopoly on supplying OEM tubeless tyres to Italian manufacturers in 1984 and 1985, and these tyres did little to enhance the handling of any motorcycle. While they did give acceptable wet weather performance, the wide Michelin A48 also contributed to heavy steering. Some Le Mans 1000 were fitted with superior Pirelli Phantom MT29 and MT28 tyres, although these were never popular in wet weather countries (like Holland). Some Le Mans 1000 owners experimented with other makes of tyre and, in many cases, a different tyre answered criticism of the 16 inch front wheel.

A steering damper remained on the right, but was almost impossible to adjust as the adjuster was located under the fairing side panel. This was another inferior quality item; not hydraulic and not durable. To improve front end rigidity and stability the mudguard included an integral fork brace and spoiler.

Because of the smaller diameter front wheel the front brake discs were also reduced in size, to 270mm. These rotors were similar to those of the 850 T5, but were an improved, two-piece floating type. The disc carriers were blue/black to match the rocker covers. The front brake calipers were still Brembo 08, positioned behind the fork legs, and the brake pads Frendo 222. The front master cylinder was now of larger diameter (15mm), with a trapezoidal reservoir, incorporating the starter and engine stop switches. It wasn't the perfect solution, and another example of hasty development, but the integrated brakes remained excellent as before. The flat-type rear disc required a new rear axle, and the rear brake caliper was located underneath the swingarm. The integral braking system was as before, but the four-way brake manifold was now neatly positioned underneath the bodywork next to the twin ignition coils.

Bodywork and controls

Most of the updates for the Le Mans 1000 were stylistic, and strongly influenced by the smaller 650 Lario. Swoops replaced angles, and the rear panels incorporated passenger handgrips. Side cover decals replaced the earlier badges, the taillight was incorporated in the rear seat unit, and the moulded seat superseded by a foam type. The 24 litre fuel tank was similar in shape to the Le Mans III example, as were the handlebar-mounted top fairing and fixed side panels. Gold-winged eagle decals continued on the fuel tank. Colours were either red or white.

Although the 16 inch front wheel came in for some criticism, the stouter front fork was a welcome improvement. The semi-floating front brake discs were smaller at 270mm.

European models incorporated the front triangular (TRIOM) turn signal indicators in the fairing, whilst US examples featured rectangular CEV turn signals on stalks. Completing the style was a rectangular headlight (finally, a 55/60 watt), and a colour-matched belly pan under the sump. Also a feature of other Italian motorcycles of this period, this belly pan was a example of style over function, and had the added disadvantage of making oil filter changes even more laborious.

Although the instrument panel – with the same instruments and warning lights – was carried over from the 850 Le Mans III, the switches were again revised. These CEV Domino switches were similar to those of the 850 T5 but of a slightly improved design. Integrating the switches and levers, they were still strange and cumbersome, the indicator on the left flicking up for right-hand turns and down for left. Horn and light switch were also on the left, and the right switch included starter and engine stop, and was integral with the front brake master cylinder. Completing the handlebar controls was a set of large and clumsy clutch and brake levers, the poorly-designed clutch pivot point requiring greater clutch effort than on earlier models. The clutch cable free play adjuster was also more difficult to use. While Moto Guzzi didn't get much right with the controls, the foam handgrips were a welcome addition, as were the dual Fiamm horns.

After frame number VV 12631 there was a new wiring loom. The riding position differed to that of

The instrument panel was carried over from the Le Mans III. This example has the updated voltmeter, but still the air-assisted Sebac fork dampers.

the Le Mans III with footpegs higher (40mm below the swingarm pivot), and further back (50mm ahead of the swingarm pivot).

In most respects the Le Mans 1000 continued the Moto Guzzi tradition, with many good quality detail touches (such as the milled footpeg supports). Unfortunately, despite a claimed dry weight of 215kg, the Le Mans 1000 was no longer a low, lean motorcycle in the style of the first Le Mans. Wet weight was considerably greater than claimed; when *Cycle* magazine, in March 1986, weighed its test bike it was 245.2kg (540.5lb). Performance of the larger engine was found to be remarkably similar to that of the 850 Le Mans III, with a standing quarter mile covered in 12.48 seconds at 109.46mph (176kph). *Motociclismo*, in October 1985, also found that the Le Mans 1000 performed similarly to the 850, managing a top speed of 217kph (135mph).

But the Le Mans 1000 still represented good value for money, and, in the US, was comparable to a Japanese 750 at a price of $4685. There was a new UK distributor for 1985: Three Cross Motorcycles in Dorset, which listed the Le Mans 1000 at £3999.

The Le Mans 1000 didn't meet with universal acceptance. Traditional Guzzi owners and many road testers weren't enamoured with the 16 inch front wheel, complaining of instability. I tested one of the first Le Mans 1000s in 1985 and, while there was weave at higher speeds, this could have been induced by the handlebar-mounted fairing as much as the 16 inch front wheel. Certainly, the Le Mans 1000 didn't have the poise of the 850 Le Mans, but my overriding recollection of the test was the discomfort caused by the incredibly strong throttle return springs rather than steering instability. Although possibly underdeveloped, the Le Mans 1000 was built in reasonable numbers for 1984 and 1985, with 2226 produced during this period.

White was offered as an alternative to red in 1984 and 1985. The frame was still black with red lower rails. (Courtesy Moto Guzzi)

The Le Mans 1000 retained the milled footpeg supports.

Le Mans 1000 second series 1986-88 (from VIN VV 100165)

Almost immediately there were complaints about the stability of the Le Mans 1000, and for 1986 a kit was offered with revised steel triple clamps. According to a factory telex to a distributor shown to me in 1987, this 1986 update reduced the trail to 90mm; period technical bulletins substantiated this update. As ride height was altered, a new, 25mm longer side stand was provided with the kit, also including a new red or white front mudguard. Although many distributors fitted this kit as standard, it wasn't long before the factory kit was officially installed. This was intended for the second series Le Mans 1000, beginning after VIN VV 100165 in early 1986. The Le Mans 1000 engine was essentially as before, but the valve covers were sometimes plain aluminium, matching the engine and transmission. In 1986, a thicker walled gudgeon pin was introduced, with a 14mm bore instead of 15mm.

As most of the criticism of the Le Mans 1000 was levelled at the chassis, it was here that most of the updates appeared. The flatter top triple clamp of the earlier kit was standard, but now of aluminium instead of steel, and accompanied by a new, lower triple clamp and spacers and revised steering damper brackets. These provided less offset, increasing the trail to 108mm and reducing the wheelbase to 1485mm. There was a new side stand, and the frame and swingarm were still black with red lower frame tubes.

Accompanying the steering geometry updates were improved Bitubo sealed dampers for the 40mm fork, and these were no longer air-assisted. Compression damping was claimed to be lighter with the Bitubo, but the ride was still harsh at lower speeds. Fitting of the Bitubo dampers didn't coincide exactly with VIN 100165, and there was

END OF THE LINE: LE MANS 1000

Le Mans 1000 distinguishing features first series 1984-85 (from frame number VV 11111)

Cylinder head received larger valves (47mm intake and 40mm exhaust)
Larger combustion chamber
High domed, three-ring 10.0:1 pistons
B10 performance camshaft
Black valve covers
Dell'Orto PHM 40ND and S dark grey carburettors
22mm carburettor float bowl retaining nut
Carburettor clamps black-painted with new tightening arrangement
Carburettors included choke and right angle cable connector
Updated engine breather with oil return from the frame to the valve covers
Black chrome-plated exhaust system with large pressed steel crossover
Full circle exhaust collars
New clutch plate design
Thinner gauge wire gearshift spring
New gearshift detent mechanism
Steering head longer and strengthened
Frame painted black with red lower frame tubes
Wider (130mm) swingarm
40mm front fork with Paioli dampers
Sebac fork dampers during 1985
Front mudguard incorporated fork brace and spoiler
Koni P7640 337mm shock absorbers
MT2.50x16 inch front wheel
MT3.00x18 inch rear wheel
Shorter side stand
270mm semi-floating disc brakes
55/60 watt headlight
Dual Fiamm horns
Decals instead of side cover badges
Taillight incorporated in the rear seat unit
CEV Domino handlebar switches
Foam handgrips
Moulded seat replaced by foam type
New milled footpeg supports
New wiring loom after frame number VV 12631
Colour choice of red or white

The 1000cc engine was virtually unchanged for 1986, sometimes retaining black valve covers.

Pirelli radial tyres were fitted in 1986 to improve stability. This example is also painted in the colours of the SE, without the black engine and transmission.
(Courtesy Two Wheels)

some equipment overlap as earlier Sebac supplies were utilized.

With the updated fork came a new generation radial tyre – a Pirelli MP7R – but, as the wheels were unchanged, the advantage of stiffer and narrower

Moto Guzzi Sport & Le Mans Bible

sidewalls that radial tyres offered was lost: to achieve maximum effect a radial tyre required a wider rim than the 2.50 and 3.00 inch of the Le Mans 1000. The lower fork legs were painted red only this year, and there was a longer, red front mudguard. Rubber mounts were added to the front mudguard brace, with 11mm mounting holes instead of 9mm to eliminate poor alignment during assembly. Although the braking system was unchanged, later rear brakes had a steel insert in the aluminium caliper support.

Although the handlebar-mounted fairing was probably contributing to instability, instead of modifying the design (this would wait until the new 1988 series), Moto Guzzi tried a short-term solution of installing black-painted steel weights in the ends of the clip-on handlebars. New Vitaloni rear view mirrors also attached to handlebar switch blocks on each side. While the bodywork was unchanged from 1985, side cover attachment was now by pins and small holders, rather than bolts and nuts. The instrument panel also included a larger voltmeter – 33mm instead of 27mm – with a different dial face. Colours were mostly red, but, as the Special Edition was produced concurrently, some had the red and white colour scheme of this model, which also had a red seat and were visually similar to the SE.

A great deal of the criticism of the Le Mans 1000 concerned the 16 inch front wheel, and during 1987

The instrument panel was basically unchanged for 1986. The forks have Bitubo dampers without air valves, and there were new weights in the handlebar ends. The awkward handlebar switches remained.

an 18 inch front wheel was available as an option. Possibly due to a negative reaction to the 16 inch front wheel, the Le Mans 1000 was not as popular as the 850cc versions. Although 1179 examples were produced in 1986, only 754 were built in 1987 with a final 71 in 1988. Most 1988 models were factory-fitted with the 18 inch front wheel, but retained the frame-mounted fairing and earlier front mudguard shape.

The Le Mans 1000 specification was inconsistent in 1986. This example has the SE colours, with a grey engine, transmission, and footpeg supports. (Courtesy Moto Guzzi)

END OF THE LINE: LE MANS 1000

By 1988 Moto Guzzi was fitting an 18 inch front wheel to the Le Mans 1000, retaining the handlebar-mounted fairing. (Courtesy Two Wheels)

Le Mans 1000 SE (Special Edition)

As a commemorative model to celebrate twenty years of the V7, a Special Edition Le Mans 1000 was released during 1986. Although listed in 1986, the model was sold into 1987 and also 1988 in the US.

In 1988 the Special Edition was the only Le Mans available in the US, and the price was very high at $6955. The US Special Edition was the first Moto Guzzi without a headlight on/off switch, and this version also had leaner carburettor jetting and a different headlight and turn signals. Just 100 examples were available in the US, with similar numbers available in other markets. Some of the US versions arrived badly corroded, and were subsequently sold at a discounted price of $4500. All Special Edition Le Mans were red/white, with a red seat, and most had a black engine and gearbox, although some earlier European examples featured a plain aluminium engine. Those with a black engine had black-painted lower frame rails and black footpeg supports. The Special Edition featured a red 'Le Mans' decal on the lower fairing, red-winged

A 1988 Le Mans 1000 with the Sydney Opera House in the background. (Courtesy Two Wheels)

Le Mans 1000 distinguishing features second series 1986-88 (from VIN VV 1000165)

Some valve covers plain aluminium in colour
Thicker gudgeon pin introduced
Flatter triple clamps to increase trail
New brackets for steering damper
Longer front mudguard with rubber mounts for steering brace
Longer side stand
Bitubo front fork dampers introduced (without air-assistance)
18 inch front wheel option during 1987 and into 1988
Later rear brakes had steel insert in the aluminium caliper support
Wider rear mudguard
New voltmeter
Steel weights in handlebar ends
New Vitaloni rear view mirrors
Side cover attachment to tail section by pins instead of bolts

eagle tank decals, and a red 'GUZZI' decal on the side panels.

But for the colours and straight cut, close ratio gearbox, there was little to differentiate the SE from the regular Le Mans 1000. This gearbox had a completely new set of ratios, differing also to the earlier Le Mans race kit. The primary ratio was 18/23, with 1st gear 17/28; 2nd 21/24; 3rd 32/21; 4th 25/19, and 5th 27/19. With 4th almost identical to the previous 5th gear, this gearbox (with the standard 7/33 final drive) offered considerably higher and closer gearing than the regular Le Mans 1000. As expected, such high gearing hurt drag strip acceleration, and *Motorcyclist* magazine in May 1988 achieved a standing quarter mile in 13.59 seconds at a speed of 102.2mph (164kph).

Le Mans 1000 CI 1988 (first series from frame number VV 14000-VV16349)

Fortunately, Moto Guzzi took heed of complaints

The Le Mans 1000 SE generally featured a black engine and transmission. The tyres were also usually Pirelli radials, not the Michelin variety as on this publicity example. (Courtesy Moto Guzzi)

END OF THE LINE: LE MANS 1000

The Le Mans 1000 SE colour scheme was attractive and distinctive. (Courtesy Two Wheels)

Le Mans 1000 SE distinguishing features

Most with black engine and transmission
Black exhaust system
Black footpeg supports
Close ratio straight cut gearbox
Red and white colour scheme with a red seat
Different decals
Black lower frame rails
Bitubo fork dampers
Pirelli radial tyres

about the Le Mans 1000 and designed an improved version during 1987. This was homologated in January 1988 as the Le Mans 1000 CI, but was commonly referred to as the Le Mans V (although, as with the Le Mans IV, this wasn't an official designation).

With the new Le Mans 1000 the sporting Moto Guzzi concept progressed, though in many respects it still didn't offer any significant advances over the earlier 850s. The engine specification was unchanged from the previous Le Mans 1000, and this was to be the final version of the big valve unit. The new Le Mans retained some links with the past, including the same dual-point distributor rather than the electronic ignition as on some other big twins (notably the SP III) introduced at around the same time. The Le Mans was also restyled, with a range of bold and striking colour schemes.

Just like the first Le Mans, the 1988 Le Mans 1000 styling was aggressive and unapologetic. As on the earlier version, while there was an official new frame number series beginning at VV 14000, many examples included a 17 digit VIN beginning with ZGUVV. Engine numbers continued the VV series and, for 1988, engine specification was essentially unchanged.

Another modification was a new series of carburettors. Although the jetting remained the same, there was a new choke arrangement with a straight, instead of right-angled, cable connection. Choke cables were now connected to both carburettors, actuated by a single cable via a two-into-one junction and left handlebar lever, which was a much more satisfactory arrangement than the earlier, low-mounted choke lever on the left. The earlier choke was also not very progressive in action – either on or off – and the new arrangement allowed for a setting in any position; particularly advantageous in cooler climates.

The starter motor was a smaller French Valeo item; an improvement as the planetary gear reduction design made it more efficient and effective when starting the big twin. The Valeo starter also had a smaller black plastic cover for the solenoid. Engines and transmission were either grey, for red and black models, or black for red, white and black examples. Most exhaust systems were black chrome this year, with red ends to the mufflers. Many final drive housings were also black but, as always, there was a degree of inconsistency, with some examples with grey engines and transmissions fitted with black final drives. Red-painted versions were fitted with plain chrome exhaust systems (also with red-ended mufflers).

While the frame was also basically the same, colour was either all black, with black lower frame rails, or all red for red examples. The steering head angle was still 28 degrees, and mounts were included on the steering head to support the fairing. The Neiman steering lock remained. There was a new, Marzocchi-built, 40mm front fork, more sophisticated than before and still with the 180mm fork tube spacing. The lower fork legs were painted two different colours: black, or pearly white to match bodywork colours. Most red examples had grey-painted fork legs.

There were new Bitubo dampers, now with a rebound damping adjuster at the top of the fork tube. As the fork offset was the same as for the 16 inch front wheel, the fork tubes were factory-set 25.4mm (one inch) above the top triple clamp. The upper and lower fork springs were unchanged, but spring preload was adjusted externally at the top by a 32mm hex nut. The steering damper was unchanged, although the attachment to the frame was revised.

The twin Koni, 337mm rear shock absorbers stayed the same, as did the rear wheel, but an 18 inch front wheel replaced the unpopular 16 inch version. The wheels were still red with polished rims, but on white examples were painted pearl white. Although the rim sizes remained at 2.50 and

Along with the frame-mounted fairing were bold new colours for the Le Mans 1000 CI. The first model had triangular, integral front turn signals. (Courtesy Moto Guzzi)

The choke on the carburettor was a straight fitting for the Le Mans 1000 CI, with the choke lever on the handlebar.

3.00 inches, smaller section tyres were fitted as Tonti believed this improved handling. These were generally tube-type Pirelli Phantoms; an MT29 100/90V18 on the front, and MT28 120/90V18 on the rear. The 18 inch front wheel was accompanied by a new front mudguard, still with a metal brace, but with the front section flared around the fork legs. Unfortunately, Moto Guzzi retained the small diameter (270mm) discs, which limited ultimate braking power. The Le Mans did finally receive the four-way brake proportioning valve, instead of the simpler four-way manifold, which had first appeared on the SP 1000 back in 1979. There was an improved front brake master cylinder, with a rectangular reservoir instead of the trapezoidal variety. The master cylinder was also free-standing, and not incorporated with the handlebar switches. With a 13mm piston and low friction pushrod between lever and piston, this was a significant improvement over the earlier type, giving similar braking power with less effort.

Moto Guzzi Sport & Le Mans Bible

Along with the 18 inch front wheel, the most noticeable improvement over the previous Le Mans 1000 was the fairing. In three pieces, with a front connecting brace, the fairing was now rigidly mounted to the frame and steering head, and supported the 170x110mm, 60/55 watt rectangular headlight. The two lower panels blended with the earlier belly pan to give the look of a one-piece full fairing. Although the instruments and dashboard were still located on the top triple clamp, turning with the handlebars, steering was considerably improved. The earliest fairings still included the triangular turn signals, but this was soon changed to rectangular TRIOM turn signals on stalks installed on a black plastic triangular block. With these indicators was an updated supporting bracket.

Apart from their colour, the steel fuel tank and rear and side body panels were unchanged from the previous Le Mans 1000. The seat was similar; either black with red pinstriping, or red with a white pinstripe, on multi-coloured versions including a white 'Le Mans' designation on each side.

Three colour schemes were initially offered: metallic black with diagonal red stripes, pearl white with red and black stripes, or traditional red. The black and red was striking, with a black seat, winged eagle tank decals, and a grey engine and transmission. The pearl white version was flashier and more daring, with a red seat and front mudguard, matching pearl white fork legs, a black engine and transmission, and a white 'GUZZI' designation on each side of the fairing. For the traditionalist the Le Mans 1000 was also available in plain red, with a grey engine and transmission, grey fork legs, and a silver chrome exhaust system. The black seat didn't feature 'Le Mans'

For 1988 the upper frame section was in three pieces. (Courtesy Moto Guzzi)

The Le Mans 1000 CI featured improved handlebar switches. On 1988 and '89 versions the fork legs sat above the triple clamp. (Courtesy Two Wheels)

designations, and the tank and side panel decals were carried over from the earlier model.

The dashboard, with dominant, white-faced Veglia tachometer, was the same but did include a new plate to attach to the top triple clamp. And while the clip-on handlebars were also as before, still with weights in the ends, the Le Mans finally received functional handlebar switches. An Italian copy of Japanese switches fitted to contemporary Hondas (such as the VFR750 and NX650), these were now free standing and featured more conventional controls. The right side was integral with the throttle but separate from the Brembo brake master cylinder. The left side light switch was considerably improved, with an orange flasher switch and push-to-cancel turn signals. Accompanying these new switches were black dogleg brake and clutch levers, a choke lever incorporated in the clutch lever bracket, and new, round, black Vitaloni rear vision mirrors (which were still not very effective, providing limited rear vision and suffering from vibration).

As the engine was the same as that in the previous Le Mans 1000, overall performance was similar. *Performance Bikes* magazine tested a black and red Le Mans 1000 in July 1988, achieving a top speed of 133.97mph with the rider prone. While not earth shattering, this was still an impressive performance for an air-cooled twin in 1988. Although the 1000 CI was arguably the best ever incarnation of the sporting Moto Guzzi twin, only 724 were produced in 1988. Distributed by Three Cross Motorcycles in the UK the retail price was £4999.

Le Mans 1000 CI 1989 (second series)

The Le Mans 1000 continued in production in limited numbers during 1989, with only a few minor updates. In April 1989, from engine number VV 16375, there was another solution to overcome the problem of spline wear on the input transmission shaft, which included a new clutch plate and input hub with deeper splines (now 4mm instead of 2mm, providing twice the contact area). Although this update was a significant improvement, unfortunately, the clutch plates were still riveted and so it failed to address the problem of rivets loosening on the plate. At around the same time, from engine number VV 16418, a spring-loaded, self-adjusting cam chain tensioner was fitted. From engine number VV 16818 there was also a new sump oil filler plug which could be removed by hand instead of requiring a 22mm wrench.

The most obvious update for 1989 was the revised fairing. Although the same shape as before (it looked identical), the top section was subdivided to incorporate the cross brace and was more rigid as the centre brace was located in the middle instead of at each end. The lower sections and belly pan were unchanged, as was the instrument panel. All the front turn signal indicators were on stalks but during the year changed to CEV. Shared with some Ducatis of this era, the CEV indicators were not only slightly differently-shaped but also included 10 watt instead of 21 watt bulbs.

There was a rationalisation of colours for 1989. The garish, pearl white option disappeared, but the distinctive red, and black with white highlighting, remained. This version retained the black frame and exhaust system, but with a grey engine and transmission. The traditional red model featured a red frame, grey fork legs, and a chrome exhaust. A new colour became available this year as a limited edition: all black with a black engine and exhaust and gold-painted wheels. The tank decals were also gold, and the seat had 'Le Mans' lettering. Production during 1989 was also modest with only 720 examples produced. UK retail stayed the same but the price of a Le Mans 1000 CI in the US was $7995.

Le Mans 1000 CI 1988 distinguishing features (first series from frame number VV 14000-VV16349)

Valeo starter motor
New Dell'Orto PHM 40N carburettors with straight choke connectors
Smaller Tudor 12V 23Ah battery
Red or black frame incorporating a fairing mount on the steering head
Frame-mounted, three-piece fairing initially with triangular turn signals
After a short time the front turn signals were rectangular TRIOM with new supports
New 40mm front fork with Bitubo dampers and rebound damping adjustment
Rebound and spring preload adjustment provided on the top of the fork
Fork tubes set 25.4mm above the top triple clamp
Revised steering damper frame attachment
2.50x18 inch front wheel
New front mudguard
Four-way integrated brake proportioning valve instead of simpler four-way manifold
Rectangular reservoir 13mm front brake master cylinder
270mm discs finished in black rather than blue
Black seat with red pinstripe or red seat with white pinstripe
Black footpeg supports
New dashboard mounting plate
Japanese-style Italian-built handlebar switches
Choke lever on clutch lever bracket
Black dogleg clutch and brake levers
New Vitaloni rear view mirrors
Red bodywork with grey engine and chromed exhaust system
Red and black bodywork (with black front mudguard, belly pan, fork legs, seat, grey engine)
White, black and red bodywork (red front mudguard, belly pan, and seat, white fork legs, black engine)

Le Mans 1000 CI 1990 (third series from frame number VV 16350-VV 16994)

Sometimes called the Le Mans 1000 Mark V NT (New Type), this was to be the final incarnation of a great line of larger capacity, sporting Moto Guzzi V-twins.

Le Mans 1000 CI 1989 distinguishing features (second series)

New clutch plate and input hub with deeper splines (from VV 16375)
Spring-loaded, self-adjusting cam chain tensioner (from VV 16418)
New engine sump oil filler plug (from VV 16818)
Revised five-piece fairing
Colour options of red, black, or red, white and black.
Black version had gold wheels
Some with CEV 10 watt turn signal indicators

The fairing was revised slightly for 1989, although retaining the same shape. The 18 inch front wheel and small 270mm front discs continued through until the end of the series.

A limited edition colour scheme for 1989 was black and gold. (Courtesy Two Wheels)

Produced in small numbers from 1990 until 1992, some minor engine updates occurred during this period. During 1991, from engine number VV 17817 there was a higher capacity oil pump, also shared with other 1000cc twins (this also included a new oil pump driving gear). The oil pump gears were 16mm instead of 14mm. This oil pump update was accompanied by a revision to the oil pan with a larger diameter internal oil passage between the pickup screen and pump (11mm instead of 8mm).

While the engines and transmissions were all now grey, some of this series were fitted with the close ratio transmission of the Le Mans 1000 SE, done for certain markets at the request of importers. For these markets the Le Mans was factory-fitted with a close ratio gearbox and higher ratio final drive.

Also new this year was a transmission oil filler plug with a 10mm Allen bolt that was no longer magnetic. The final drive (also grey this year) received a revised, non-magnetic, drain plug. All the mufflers were bright chrome, now with black ends instead of red. Most alternators were also a Spanish Saprisa on this third series. The Saprisa alternator was fitted to other 1000cc twins from 1987 (such as the SP II and California III), but immediately began to cause problems. The Saprisa rotor contained only magnets, and, although this was an improvement as they didn't disintegrate, the Saprisa alternator wasn't as efficient at charging at low engine speeds. If the engine was run at slow engine speeds for prolonged periods, this resulted in battery problems, and was a particular difficulty in countries like the US where the headlight came on when the ignition was switched on.

Another side effect of excessive low revs was the clutch plate rivets loosening. According to Ivar de Gier, during 1990, Moto Guzzi began to take the Saprisa alternators from the existing stock of California IIIs and fit them to the Le Mans because it believed that the more sporting nature of this model would mean it would not give rise d to these charging problems.

Although the basic style of the Le Mans 1000 CI stayed the same, there were some noticeable chassis and equipment updates for 1990. The frame – still in red or black – included a revised steering head lock arrangement, with the plunger at the front for the ignition key activated steering lock. The five-piece fairing was unchanged, but included a new steering head bracket that also supported the updated instrument panel. The instrument layout featured the same tachometer and voltmeter as before, but a new speedometer. The warning light panel was new, too, and included a separate, hazed warning switch and light; a headlight adjustment switch was also incorporated. Although no change to the controls, the weights in the handlebar ends were smaller and lighter.

The front fork was new and incorporated 25mm longer fork tubes, and correspondingly longer steering stem. Upper and lower fork springs were longer, as was the damper. In 1991, Moto Guzzi began fitting plastic buffers inside the bottom of the fork tubes, refining fork action at full compression under heavy braking.

A classic red with chrome exhaust Le Mans 1000 CI was also available in 1988. (Courtesy Moto Guzzi)

END OF THE LINE: LE MANS 1000

For 1990 the Le Mans 1000 received a new instrument panel with a different speedometer and warning light layout. (Courtesy Ivar de Gier)

Moto Guzzi Sport & Le Mans Bible

There was considerable inconsistency in the supply and fitting of many ancillary components during this period as Moto Guzzi used up existing stock and was reluctant to order new supplies. Some examples were so badly finished that they left the factory with vital components completely missing!

Colour options were now red or black, the red examples with red frames and red wheels with polished rims as before. Black versions had a black frame and white-milk wheels. They also had gold decals, and white striping on the seat.

The Le Mans 1000 was available in the US at $7995 in 1990, but was not listed for 1991. In the UK, the Le Mans 1000 retailed at £5600 in 1990 and £5999 in 1991. Production was extremely modest; just 325 produced in 1990, 147 in 1991, and 143 in 1992. Many of these remained unsold and some were converted to the *Ultima Edizione*.

Le Mans 1000 Ultima Edizione

Although the 1990 version of the Le Mans 1000 was an excellent motorcycle, as there was so little new in its specification (it could almost have been produced ten years earlier), demand was virtually non-existent by 1992.

Performance was quite similar to that of the

Le Mans 1000 CI distinguishing features 1990 (third series from frame number VV16350-VV 16994)

Saprisa alternator
Higher capacity oil pump with 16mm gears and new oil pump driving gear (from engine number VV 17817)
Oil pan with 11mm oil passage between the pickup screen and pump
Some examples with close ratio transmission
Non-magnetic, final drive filler plug with 10mm Allen head
Frame (red or black) with front steering lock mount
New fairing support brackets
New speedometer
New instrument panel
Ignition key incorporating steering lock
Headlight height adjuster on dashboard
Smaller and lighter handlebar inserts
25mm longer fork tubes and steering stem
Longer upper and lower fork springs, and a longer damper
From 1991 plastic buffers fitted inside the bottom of the fork tubes
Colour options of all-red or all-black (with white wheels)

The Ultima Edizione Le Mans was created out of existing stock during 1993. Here, it's shown at the Amsterdam Show of 1992 where it was launched. (Courtesy Ivar de Gier)

first Le Mans 850 of 1976, and sporting motorcycles had moved beyond the world of the twin rear shock absorbers and Brembo 08 twin-piston brake calipers. In comparison with the new generation Ducati 888, Honda Fireblade, Yamaha FZR, or Suzuki GSX-R, the Le Mans was considered an anachronism. Fashion called for smaller diameter wheels and wider tyres, and the Le Mans was tall and heavy, and didn't produce enough horsepower. The motorcycle community at large regarded it as a relic from the past, and the traditional Moto Guzzi enthusiast baulked at its plastic bodywork.

Although Le Mans production was almost at a standstill, during 1991 and 1992 the factory warehouse was full of unsold machines. Ivar de Gier remembers large numbers of Le Mans awaiting completion, many without seats. "Four months later they were still there without seats, some taken apart for spares. I felt it was such a sad end to a great bike. The Mark V was really a much better bike than the Mark IV, but totally unappreciated."

With the four-valve Daytona about to supersede it, and the big-valve engine finally failing to meet new emission requirements, an end to Le Mans production was imminent. Deciding not to remake the model with the new 1000cc twin used on the 1000S, the factory faced a dilemma about what to do with the existing stock. Fortunately, help was at hand.

In 1991, Moto Guzzi released its first anniversary model, the 70th California III. Not available until 1992, this commemorative model featured a brown leather

END OF THE LINE: LE MANS 1000

seat, special paint, a badge on the front mudguard, a numbered plate on the steering head, and a certificate signed by De Tomaso and managing director, Paolo Donghi. The recipe was incredibly successful, and the 70th Anniversary California sold out immediately.

In a discussion with the Netherlands and Benelux Moto Guzzi distributor, Greenib, in June 1992, Ivar de Gier mentioned the success of the 70th Anniversary California, suggesting Moto Guzzi repeat this with the Le Mans. This idea met with a positive reception in Mandello, and in October 1992 the *Ultima Edizione* Le Mans was officially launched at the RAI International Motorcycle Show in Amsterdam.

Painted either black or red (to establish an association with the new Daytona), each model came with a certificate signed by De Tomaso and Donghi, and an individually numbered copper plate on the top triple clamp. The certificate was printed in the language of the country of sale, and specification was as for the final 1000cc Le Mans (the only update was that some markets received a 350 watt Ducati alternator (as fitted to the later 1000 S) instead of the Saprisa item). This change also required a new crankshaft with a keyed, straight shaft instead of the earlier tapered shaft. Cosmetically, there were few changes from the final 1000 Le Mans. Existing Le Mans machines at the factory were disassembled and repainted; on red examples the fork legs were painted red, and the wheels were red without polished rims.

Some examples of the Ultima Edizione were created out of existing stock, but 54 were built in 1993. The total produced was 99, and number 99 was given to the Dutch importer, Greenib, in recognition of its input into the model's creation. Although no longer the Dutch Moto Guzzi importer, this machine is still on display in Greenib's Warmond showroom.

1000 S/SE

As seen with the creation of the Le Mans Ultima Edizione, Moto Guzzi was easily influenced by distributors when it came to producing certain models. In 1987, the German importer, A&G Motorrad, persuaded Moto Guzzi to create the Mille GT, a new, standard style 1000cc twin with strong nostalgic connotations. This was largely a 'parts bin special' but was successful enough for A&G to request another specific retro version in 1989, the 1000 S.

Retro models are now a mainstream component in motorcycle line-ups but this wasn't the case in 1989. Many manufacturers today are producing nostalgic retro motorcycles as niche models in an endeavour to expand market share. But Moto Guzzi was the first, and in this respect the 1000 S was many years ahead of its time. The styling impetus for the 1000 S came from the shortlived 750 S and 750 S3 of 1974 and 1975, one of Moto Guzzi's outstanding stylist creations. Continuing until 1993, the 1000 S came to represent the end of a twenty-two year line of Tonti-framed sporting Moto Guzzis.

1000 S first series 1990-91 (from frame number VV 50001-VV 51190, engine numbers in VV series)

With an amalgam of parts from various models, the 1000 S could almost be considered yet another 'parts bin special.'

Although the 1000 S was styled to resemble the 750 S3, the basic engine and chassis were shared with the Le Mans 1000. The first series of 1990-91 featured the big-valve, 1000cc engine, with higher performance camshaft, Dell'Orto PHM 40N carburettors (with the same jetting), and twin point distributor. Sharing the VV engine number series with the Le Mans, this 1000 S had a Bosch alternator and Valeo starter. Some 1991 examples had a Saprisa alternator, and from engine number VV 50625, there was a new, higher capacity oil pump and matching drive sprocket. Although top speed of the 1000 S was not significantly higher than that of the original 750 S, the 81 horsepower motor provided considerably better on-the-road performance. The exhaust system, with upswept mufflers, was bright chrome-plated with black ends on the mufflers.

The 1000 S also came with polished rocker covers, chrome-plated engine protection bars, and large rectangular, chrome rear vision mirrors. US versions featured the usual different carburettor jetting and headlight.

But for the straight rear subframe, the frame of the 1000 S was identical to the Le Mans'. Contrary to some reports, the swingarm was identical to that of the Le Mans 1000, black versions carrying the same part number. The revised rear subframe allowed for a classic, straight dual seat in the style of the 750 S and S3. The 24 litre steel fuel tank was also the same shape as on the earlier 750 and Le Mans,

---

Le Mans 1000 Ultima Edizione distinguishing features 1993

Signed plate on the top triple clamp
Certificate signed by De Tomaso and Tonti
Some versions with a Ducati alternator and updated crankshaft
Chrome-plated exhaust system
Red or black versions produced
Red wheels without polished rims
Red-painted fork legs on red examples

The 1000S was one of the first of the now popular retro bikes, designed to recreate the styling of the earlier 750 S and 750 S3. (Courtesy Two Wheels)

A popular option on the 1000 S was wire-spoked wheels. (Courtesy Moto Guzzi)

with a locking lid (as on the Le Mans II). The tank featured white metal 'MOTO GUZZI' badges; vented side covers replicating those of the 750 S and S3 continued the retro look.

The 40mm fork with adjustable Bitubo damper and Koni shock absorbers also came from the Le Mans. The 180mm fork was the same as on the 1990 Le Mans, with longer fork tubes, and the lower legs were polished aluminium. The 270mm, semi-floating disc brakes, and linked braking system with proportioning valve, was from the Le Mans, but the 1000 S received new stainless steel mudguards, the front very abbreviated.

The grey-painted, 18 inch wheels were as for the Le Mans 1000 CI, with rim widths of 2.50 and 3.00 inches, although a popular later option was a set of traditional Akront wire-spoked wheels. These required different fork legs, and the spoked wheels included narrower rims: 2.15 inch on the front and 2.50 inch on the rear. The rims were Spanish Akront light alloy, but not lipped as on the earlier Borrani, while the hubs were similar in design to those on the original 750 S, incorporating 40 straight-pull, stainless steel spokes. Both types of wheel were shod with

END OF THE LINE: LE MANS 1000

Pirelli Phantom MT29 and MT28 tyres, as on the Le Mans 1000 CI.

While the clip-on handlebars, black levers, and Italian-made, Japanese-style switches also came from the Le Mans 1000 CI, the plastic instrument panel – with white-faced 70mm Veglia speedometer and tachometer – derived from the V65 SP; layout was similar to that of the earlier 850 T3. There was a central ignition switch (without steering lock), and seven warning lights. The handgrips were no longer foam rubber, and a 170mm, round, 60/55 watt CEV headlight sat on nicely-milled aluminium fork brackets. The rectangular taillight also sat on a separate steel bracket in the style of earlier bikes, while the dual Fiamm horns were shared with the Le Mans 1000. Completing the 750 S and S3 retro look was a similar colour scheme. Unlike the three colours of the original, the 1000 S came in black with either orange/red stripes, or black with green stripes, which was set apart by a green frame and swingarm.

During 1990, the instrument panel was updated with a polished, stainless steel plate supporting the white-faced Veglia instruments, plus some small additional lights for turn signals neutral, high beam, oil pressure, and alternator charge. This instrument set-up also used different cables. Although the 1000 S styling received universal acclaim, this didn't translate into volume sales. Production levels were always low, with only 524 built in 1990, and 401 in 1991. In 1990, the UK price was £5499, rising to £5899 in 1991.

With no Moto Guzzi models distributed in the US during 1991, the 1000 S wasn't initially available there. Maserati/Moto Guzzi moved from Baltimore to Lillington, North Carolina, at this time and became known as Moto America. While Europe received the updated, smaller valve 1000 S for 1992, the big-valve version arrived in the US for the 1992 model year priced at $9350.

1000 SE 1991

While the German importer, A&G Motorrad, was responsible for the impetus to produce the 1000 S that was eventually available worldwide, British importer, Three Cross, persuaded Moto Guzzi to produce a specific version for the UK: the 1000 SE (England). Available in the UK only, this model was essentially a 1000 S, painted red and incorporating a small headlight fairing (with day-glow front section) like the first 850 Le Mans. The large, round front turn signals were relocated from the headlight brackets

The second series 1000 S had a new instrument panel, with white-faced instruments in an aluminium surround.

1000 S and SE first series distinguishing features 1990-91 (from frame number VV 50001-VV 51190)

Polished rocker covers
Bosch alternator, some late versions with Saprisa Valeo starter
Chrome-plated exhaust system
Black ends on mufflers
Chrome engine guards
Frame with straight rear subframe
Frame black or green (with green stripes)
Fuel tank shaped like those of the 750 S, S3 and Le Mans
Colour options of black with green stripes, or black with red/orange stripes

White-faced Veglia speedometer and tachometer
During 1990 new stainless steel instrument panel
Round CEV headlight
Rectangular chrome rear vision mirrors
Hard rubber handgrips
Short stainless steel front mudguard
Polished aluminium top triple clamp
Wire-spoked wheels with different fork legs an option
1000 SE for UK market only
SE red with small handlebar fairing

END OF THE LINE: LE MANS 1000

to the lower triple clamp, as on the Mille GT, and wheels were wire-spoked.

The 1000 SE sold for £5999, with an option list that included an aluminium clutch basket, lightened ring gear, Lucas Rita electronic ignition, Malossi carburettors with Ram Air filters, and a Lafranconi exhaust system. With these modifications the 1000 SE was capable of 126.9mph (204.2kph) as tested by *Bike* magazine, but the price rose to over £7000. The 1000 SE was available through 1993.

1000 S second series 1992-93 (from frame number VV 60000-VV 60058; engine numbers in VN 20000 series) US version from 1993

Tighter emission controls in Europe and the US ensured the demise of the big-valve engine during 1992. Although a small number of big-valve engines were produced for the final Le Mans, the smaller valve SP III engine replaced it in the 1000 S from 1992.

These engines had numbers in the VN series of the SP III, California III and Strada 1000. Despite producing less power, in many respects this engine was an improvement over the Le Mans type as it gave more mid-range power and was less labour intensive to maintain. The combustion chamber

For 1992 the 1000 S received the smaller valve motor of the SP III.

reverted to that of the earlier 850 Le Mans, with a 44mm intake and 37mm exhaust valve, and 74mm chamber diameter with a depth of 27mm. Combined with lower compression (9.5:1) 88mm pistons and a different camshaft, this more efficient combustion chamber design allowed the engine to comply with the stricter emission regulations. The pistons were of a higher dome design than those in the CX 100, but lower domed than in the Le Mans 1000. New valves and valve seats allowed the engine to be used with unleaded fuel.

Transmission was mostly unchanged but for an additional washer on the output shaft between 5th gear and the sealing O-ring, while the 8 final drive ring gear lock plates were replaced by Schnoor washers.

On this smaller valve engine the carburettors were Dell'Orto PHF 36 DD and DS versions; US versions (from 1993, as the 1000 S wasn't sold in 1992) had different jetting. Ignition on 1992 models was an electronic Motoplat, with a preset electronic advance up to a maximum of 34-35 degrees. The electronic advance provided was somewhere between that of the Le Mans Marelli S311A, which provided a much slower advance, and the touring S311B with a steeper curve. The Motoplat soon earned a reputation for unreliability and was shortlived on the 1000 S.

For 1993 the 1000 S received a Magneti Marelli Digiplex ignition, similar to that used on the Ducati

906 Paso of 1988-89. This was more sophisticated than the Motoplat as it incorporated a vacuum sensor to allow for engine load. The distributor was replaced by a blanked-off plate, and crankshaft position was determined by a pickup mounted in a bell housing that sensed ignition from a new, lighter flywheel instead of the long distributor shaft. Vacuum hoses attached to the intake manifolds, and a central electronic processor determined ignition timing from the crank position and intake vacuum in accordance with a set of pre-mapped ignition curves. The Digiplex system also included new ignition coils.

Also new for this second series of the 1000 S was an uprated alternator, but supplied by Ducati instead of Saprisa. This Ducati 14V25 amp, 350 watt alternator required a new crankshaft with a keyed, straight shaft instead of the earlier tapered shaft. Accompanied by a not totally reliable Ducati regulator, the alternator provided improved low rpm charging. Other electrical system updates included a single round horn. Three types of battery could be fitted: a 12V 24Ah by either Fiamm or AAA, or a 12V 28Ah from Varta.

Completing the engine specification was an updated exhaust system that included a new crossover underneath the transmission, and less upswept SP III mufflers with new brackets. Unlike the hollow, Le Mans type of crossover, this included an additional muffler, or an optional catalytic converter. Although claimed power had reduced to 71 horsepower at 6800rpm, in many respects the new engine was an improvement because it was more tractable and less maintenance intensive. The biggest flaw regarding maintenance remained the inaccessible oil filter.

This series of 1000 S also featured the revised instrument panel, on a polished stainless steel bracket (though some had a black bracket). The seat had a different shape and cover. This version of the 1000 S was virtually a limited edition with just 196 produced in 1992 and 84 in 1993.

The smaller valve 1000 S didn't arrive in the US until 1993, priced at $8990. US examples featured leaner carburation and a different headlight, and most (if not all) were green, with a green frame. As it didn't prove very popular, in an effort to boost sales the 1000 S remained in the US catalogue for 1994, but fewer than 200 were sold in total. This wasn't surprising given that the 750 S (with tank stripes) and 750 S3 were never sold in the US, meaning that the 1000 S didn't generate nostalgic appeal. Even in Europe the 1000 S wasn't as successful as it should have been. Although it was a visual success, underneath the retro bodywork was a retro motorcycle. Even the final version was still rooted in the past, and it was only after production ended that demand increased for the 1000 S.

Today, this model has garnered a cult following to rival the original 750 S3. With only 1360 examples produced over five years, the 1000 S is almost as rare.

1000 S second series distinguishing features 1992-93 (from frame number VV 60000-VV 60058)

Engine numbers in the VN 2000 series
44mm intake and 37mm exhaust valves
Valves and seats compatible with unleaded fuel
Combustion chamber 74mm diameter with a depth of 27mm
9.5:1 pistons
Different camshaft
Washer installed on the output shaft between 5th gear and the sealing O-ring
8 final drive ring gear lock plates replaced by Schnoor washers
Ducati 350 watt alternator and Ducati regulator
Dell'Orto PHF 36 DD and DS carburettors
Motoplat electronic ignition
Magneti Marelli Digiplex ignition from 1993
Single horn
Exhaust crossover included an additional muffler
Mufflers less upswept
Different seat

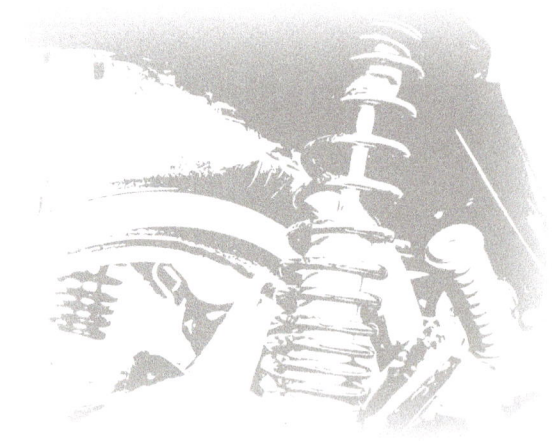

Racing the V7 Sport & Le Mans

Of the V7 Special's limited competition participation during 1969 and 1970, apart from the speed record sessions, much was unofficial. In 1969, Alessandro Gritti rode a V7 Special in the Motogiro road race, without any significant result, and in 1970 the V7 was entered in the 500 kilometre race at Monza, in which Luciano Rossi crashed. In August 1970, French importer, Charles Krajka, entered a V7 racer in the Bol d'Or at Monthléry. This machine incorporated many engine parts from the world record bikes covered in chapter 1 but, by this time, the first two prototype V7 Sports were already complete.

Another significant racing Guzzi of the period was the ZDS racer. Sponsored by ZDS, the US West Coast distributor, this bike was essentially a 1969 Ambassador insurance write-off, and was prepared specifically for the Daytona 200. Created by Bob Blair and George Kerker, it was intended to take on Harley-Davidson, but the AMA conspired to alter the regulations and the Guzzi was excluded when its protruding cylinder heads wouldn't pass a new test rig.

As the US was Guzzi's most important export market at the time, Kerker managed to obtain many of the engine parts of the 1969 world record bikes. He visited Mandello where he tested one of the record bikes. Impressed with its performance, Blair and Kerker enlisted Tonti's assistance in developing the racer.

The engine included special Norris camshafts, 10:1 Mondial pistons, and cylinder head porting by C R Axtell. Carburation was still via square-slide Dell'Orto VHB 29 carburettors, although fuel injection

Luciano Rossi on the V7 Special in the 1970 Monza 500km race. (Courtesy Ivar de Gier)

was planned. The starter motor, battery and dynamo were removed and the frame altered considerably to get the weight down to an astonishing 150kg. Rickman forks, with a single Lockheed front disc brake, were fitted, along with a 19 inch front and 18 inch rear wheel. Many other components were sourced from other racing machines, including Ducati megaphones and a Triumph fuel tank and seat.

An era of long-distance racing began when Krajka entered this V7 Special in the 1970 Bol d'Or. (Courtesy Ivar de Gier)

Unfortunately, the ZDS racer didn't get the opportunity to prove itself except in non-AMA races during 1970 and 1971, mostly in California and Texas.

Jan Kampen was also heavily involved in racing the V7 in the Netherlands. Kampen befriended Tonti shortly after he joined Guzzi, and switched to racing a V7 in 1968 after winning the Dutch production championship on a Norton twin. Tired of breaking primary and drive chains, Kampen had fond memories of racing a Guzzi 175 in the 1950s, and bought one of the first V7s, which he entered in the 1969 Zandvoort Six-hour race, finishing second. He then switched to a 757cc V7 and, with access to a dynometer at the technical university in Delft, was able to increase power to 60hp at 6800rpm.

Kampen shared much of what he learned with Tonti, and for 1970 raised the compression ratio to 10:1, installed 36mm, Amal carburettors, and achieved 65hp at 7000rpm. He next fitted a Ceriani front fork and Manx Norton brakes, but in the 1970 Zandvoort race retired with a dropped valve whilst in third place. Intent on winning the 1971 race, Kampen enlarged the engine to 810cc with Volkswagen 96mm, 9.5:1 pistons, and switched to Bing carburettors. Kampen had a Fiat car dealership, so installed Fiat valves, and built a one-off, five-speed gearbox in anticipation of achieving 70 horsepower, but the bike was badly crashed in testing prior to the 1971 Zandvoort six-hour race.

When the V7 Sport became available it was no coincidence that Kampen was able to install his racing V7 engine in the new sporting frame. According to Ivar de Gier: "It was a tight fit but it could be done. Tonti designed it with the smallest margin so it was possible. Most people don't believe it was possible to install a 'loop-frame' engine in a V7 Sport chassis, but Tonti designed it with this in mind and only requiring small changes. The ignition shaft needed to be shortened and the generator replaced by a smaller Fiat 600 car type. Two small connecting plates were also required for the lower front engine mounts. But maintenance was difficult and it was a short-term solution until the racing V7 Sport engine was developed. All this was planned, as Tonti took people that raced the V7 very seriously."

Racing the V7 Sport

During this period Tonti was busy developing the V7 Sport, primarily with racing in mind. The frame was designed along racing lines, and, when he publicly unveiled his creation on 13 June 1971 at the Monza 500 kilometre race for 750cc production machines, it created a sensation. The field of 39 included

RACING THE V7 SPORT AND LE MANS

Luciano Gazzola shared this V7 Special with Raimondo Riva at Monza in 1970. (Courtesy Ivar de Gier)

Regulations required the bikes to look like street models, complete with headlight, taillight, and full instrumentation.

This promising racing debut led to official entries in the other two 500km production races in Italy that year (Modena and Vallelunga), and the Bol d'Or 24-hour endurance race at Le Mans on 11 and 12 September. For this race the racing department – including Ing Sergio Valentini and Abrama Rollo, along with veteran racing mechanic, Ettore Casadio – prepared two 844cc, V7 Sport racers. The stroke was lengthened to 78mm, with an 83mm bore; with a pair of 35mm racing Dell'Orto carburettors, power was a claimed 70 horsepower at 7500rpm. The exhaust was an abbreviated megaphone type, the front brake a larger Fontana, and a half fairing was added to improve high speed performance. One 844 was ridden by Mandracci and Brambilla, and the other by Riva and Abbondio Sciaresa.

Mandracci and Brambilla led for more than ten hours before a broken rocker delayed them. Later, Mandracci crashed, and an hour from the end of the race the pair suffered a puncture. Surprisingly, they still finished third behind the Laverda 750 SFC of Augusto Brettoni and Bruno Cretti, and the winning BSA triple of Ray Pickrell and Percy Tait. Riva and Sciaresa finished sixth. This superb debut Le Mans result would ultimately inspire the next generation

The V7 Sport's racing debut was the 1971 Monza 500km race for series production machines. Riva and Piazzalunga finished third. (Courtesy Ivar de Gier)

Laverda, Norton, Triumph, and Honda 750s, ridden by some of the best Italian riders.

Moto Guzzi entered two V7 Sports; Vittorio Brambilla and Guido Mandracci sharing one and Raimondo Riva and Pierantonio Piazzalunga the other. After holding second place for much of the race, Riva and Piazzalunga finished third, behind the Triumph Trident of Blegi and Galtrucco, and the Honda 750 of Bonalumi and Mambretti. It was a brilliant debut, vindicating Tonti's design.

The V7 Sport racing prototype was remarkably similar to the regular Telaio Rosso. The seat was lowered, but because these races were run as a Le Mans start (where riders ran across the track to start their machines), the electric start was retained.

The V7 Sport was also raced in other Italian endurance events during 1971: this is Tavernese in the Modena 500km race. (Courtesy Ivar de Gier)

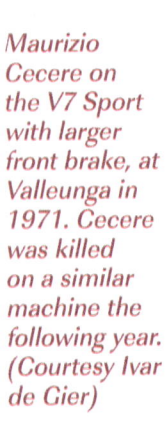

Maurizio Cecere on the V7 Sport with larger front brake, at Valleunga in 1971. Cecere was killed on a similar machine the following year. (Courtesy Ivar de Gier)

V7 Sport, the 850 Le Mans, but that was still four years away.

One week later, at Modena on the 19 September, the official 750cc V7 Sport raced again. In the 500km event Riva and Sciaresa were rated with excellent chances, but Riva was sidelined by a collision with Cereda's Laverda on the second lap. In the final 1971 long-distance production race at Vallelunga, Brambilla and Cavalli finished second behind the Laverda 750SFC of Bertorello and Loigo after their engine lost power in the final stage of the race. The V7 Sport was competitive, but the anticipated production racing results were elusive during 1971.

Moto Guzzi continued a factory racing programme during 1972. April saw the inaugural Imola 200 race for F750 machines, hugely promoted as the 'Daytona of Europe.' Nearly every major motorcycle manufacturer was represented with works machinery, and Moto Guzzi prepared a team of three special V7 Sports. These were tested at Monza prior to the race, and one of the testers – Mike Hailwood – was soon lapping as fast as Gazzola. While he was offered a ride in the Imola 200, Guzzi couldn't meet Hailwood's salary demand. When the racing bikes lined up at Imola, the drum brakes of the prototype had been replaced by triple Lockheed discs, and featured shorter exhaust pipes. Carburation was by the new 40mm Dell'Orto concentric with accelerator pumps. Three bikes were ridden by Brambilla, Jack Findlay, and Mandracci, finishing 8th, 10th, and 11th respectively, the Guzzis overshadowed by Ducati on this occasion.

Moto Guzzi also contested the 1972 Italian production long-distance series with factory and privately prepared machines. In the Monza 500 kilometre race, Ernesto and Vittorio Brambilla finished 3rd with Luciano Gazzola and Carena 7th. Sandwiched by Triumph Tridents, the Brambilla bike was one of the Imola 750 racers, with triple Lockheed disc brakes, which was later converted to a street version, with headlight and taillight, but still retaining the racing fairing. At Vallelunga in October 1972, the Brambilla brothers held first place on their privately-entered Telaio Rosso until the 120th lap before retiring with engine failure. The second Telaio Rosso of Sciaresa and Mulazzani finished second. This race was marred by the death of another Guzzi rider, Maurizio Cecere.

Also during 1972 the 844 was again raced in endurance events. At the Bol d'Or 24-hour race on September 16 and 17, Riva and Mandracci finished fourth at an average speed of 115.59mph (185.98kph) after leading for 18 hours before suffering transmission problems. Riva and Carena also rode in the 24-hours of Liège at Zolder in August.

All of these long-distance racing V7 Sports featured an enlarged fuel filler to allow for quicker refuelling during the race, and – toward the end of the season – featured twin Brembo front disc brakes.

With De Tomaso assuming control of Moto Guzzi, the scale of the official racing program was immediately reduced and the racing department decimated. During 1973 there were only a few entries in major events such as the Barcelona 24-hour race in July, where an 844cc endurance racer ridden by Riva and Luciano Gazzola finished 5th,

Vittorio Brambilla was one of the leading V7 Sport riders in Italian endurance races.
(Courtesy Ivar de Gier)

Moto Guzzi prepared three Formula 750 racers for the 1972 Imola 200. An early version, with a drum front brake, was tested at Monza. (Courtesy Moto Guzzi)

On a Formula 750 racer Jack Findlay finished 10th in the 1972 Imola 200 race. (Courtesy Ivar de Gier)

RACING THE V7 SPORT AND LE MANS

The Imola 200 racers featured triple Lockheed disc brakes and 40mm Dell'Orto carburettors. (Courtesy Ivar de Gier)

Gazzola was one of the most successful V7 Sport racers at Monza in the 1972 500km race. (Courtesy Ivar de Gier)

completing 683 laps. This special racer was fitted with double Lockheed front disc brakes but, again, the Guzzi was overshadowed by Ducati, whose 864cc prototype won the event at record speed. Guzzi's factory racer covered 683 laps compared to the Ducati's 720, but did provide the impetus for the 1975 production Le Mans.

Tonti continued to develop the 850, with the assistance of Kampen, during 1973 and 1974, the engine evolving from a V7 Sport-based unit to the newer, 750 S3 type. Kampen experimented with a front crankshaft ball bearing and a 1000cc engine, but after 1974 Tonti and Kampen reduced their racing involvement.

During 1974 the only Guzzis raced were by privateers or distributors, often with factory assistance. In the 1974 Italian 750cc production series, Sciaresa won at Monza but the V7 Sport was now outclassed by the Ducati 750 Super Sport and Laverda 750 SFC. There was no entry in Bol d'Or this year, although in the 1974 Barcelona 24-hour race Sciaresa and Mulazzani finished 4th, a result which prompted a semi-official entry in some 1975 endurance races when Sciaresa and Romeri came second at Mugello, and Duilio Agostini and Bruno Scola unsuccessfully raced in the Bol d'Or. In Italian production racing, Orlando Macchi had some success on his 850 Guzzi, dominating the Vallelunga 1000cc race in September, while Gazzola raced an 850cc V7 Sport at the Trofeo La Moto 1000 at Misano.

Racing the Le Mans

Release of the 850 Le Mans towards the end of 1975 instigated renewed interest in racing, assisted by the financial contribution of Luciano Gazzola, with the support of Tonti and factory mechanic Bruno Scola. Their work in developing the semi-official Le Mans racers led to many modifications carrying through to the production line, and they were also instrumental in the release of the official factory racing kit that was developed over the years from racing experience. As Tonti bowed out of racing, and financial pressure forced Gazzola to become a mechanic for other teams, Scola became the driving force behind the Moto Guzzi racing effort.

1976 saw further involvement in the Coupe d'Endurance with entries in the Montjuich 24-hour race and the Bol d'Or. Riva and Gazzola finished 9th at Montjuich, with Krajka Guzzis filling 15th and 16th places at the Bol d'Or. These machines displaced 1000cc and, with 40mm Dell'Orto carburettors, produced 90hp at 8500rpm.

To help promote the new model, the first Le Mans to arrive in the US was given to Reno Leoni by the Premier Corporation to prepare for a new Superbike racing class. By 1976, two-strokes had driven the four-strokes out of open class racing in America, but, as they bore no relationship to street motorcycles, the AMA created the Superbike series to woo back the fans. Superbike regulations required the machines to look standard – even with a taillight – and because stock frames were retained, this series

Abbondio Sciaresa on his way to second at Vallelunga in 1972. (Courtesy Ivar de Gier)

Gazzola on the 850cc V7 Sport at the 1975 Trofeo La Moto 1000 at Misano. (Courtesy Ivar de Gier)

Sciaresa also raced a Le Mans prototype during 1975. (Courtesy Ivar de Gier)

A semi-official racer was entered in the 1975 Bol d'Or, and ridden by Bruno Scola (astride the machine) and Duilio Agostini, with assistance from Gazzola (on the left). They didn't finish. (Courtesy Ivar de Gier)

particularly suited the European twin cylinder machines. The Japanese Superbikes were handicapped by engines that overpowered the chassis, unlike the Moto Guzzi Le Mans, Ducati Super Sport, and BMW R90S.

With vast experience of preparing Ducati racers, expatriate Italian Leoni quickly installed the factory racing kit and Koni racing shock absorbers on the Le Mans, though didn't have time to fit wider wheels and slick racing tyres. Despite this handicap, Mike Baldwin finished fifth in the inaugural Superbike race at Daytona in March 1976. This race was won by the big budget Butler & Smith BMW R90Ss, but for the next round at Loudon in June the Moto Guzzi was more competitive. Leoni installed wider rims, and the combination of Baldwin's exceptional riding and the advantage of Brembo brakes secured the Moto Guzzi Le Mans its first AMA Superbike victory. Baldwin won by a clear 16 seconds, surprising the BMW team. Throughout 1976 Leoni continued to develop the engine, fitting a Norris camshaft and 92mm pistons. He installed ball bearings for the camshaft and front crankshaft, but this first Superbike season comprised only four races. Baldwin retired with electrical problems at Laguna Seca, ending the series in fifth place. At some non-championship races the Leoni Le Mans was also successful: Kurt Liebmann won at Pocono in August, and Baldwin and Liebmann finished first and second in a 200 mile endurance race at Pocono in October. The only failure was a snapped driveshaft in a club race at Loudon.

Baldwin was back on the Leoni-tuned Le Mans for 1977, and after finishing fifth again at Daytona, won the next round at Charlotte, North Carolina, by an impressive 23 seconds. Liebmann finished second on another Le Mans. Baldwin crashed on the last lap while in the lead at Loudon and was docked a lap for receiving outside assistance from Leoni; he was credited with sixth. Baldwin managed a second at Pocono but his inconsistency lost him the championship and he finished third.

Modifications for the 1977 season included a

RACING THE V7 SPORT AND LE MANS

10.8:1 compression ratio (achieved by shortening the cylinders), custom valve guides, Leoni's own ported cylinder heads, lightened clutch (by 3.5 kilograms), a breather to vent oil back to the crankcases, and a spacer between sump and crankcases to reduce internal oil friction. Capacity returned to 850cc and power was around 90hp. Chassis updates included a notched swingarm to accommodate a Michelin SB10 rear slick tyre on a WM5 rim, 13.5 inch Koni shocks with Girling springs, and 20 weight fork oil in the stock 35mm Guzzi forks that were lowered 3-4mm in the triple clamps. A match for any other Superbike in 1977, Baldwin was timed at 143mph (230kph) at Daytona.

There was limited Guzzi involvement in the 1977 FIM Coupe d'Endurance and results were uninspiring; the highest finish in any round was 12th place achieved by the Spanish pairing of Perez Rubio and Morante at Barcelona. Stephane Heltal and D'Angelo managed 14th in the Bol d'Or on the Krajka entry, indicating that the days of the Guzzi twin seriously threatening Japanese endurance giants were over. But, as was shown in America, there was still a racing life for the Le Mans in production-based events.

Manchester rider, Roy Armstrong, surprised the pundits by winning the 1977 series of the Avon Roadrunner Production championship, for production motorcycles, backed by Avon tyres. Rules allowed chassis and engine improvements as long as the parts were freely available. Roy Armstrong rode a basically standard machine for most of the 1977 season, only installing high compression 88mm pistons, a B10 camshaft and racing valve springs toward the end of the season. Armstrong worked for Sports Motorcycles in Manchester which also entered a 950cc Le Mans for director,

John Sear. This machine included the full factory racing uprating kit and Sear finished third in the championship.

For the 1977 Isle of Man, Bruno Scola took two factory-prepared, 950cc engines to be installed in the Sports Motorcycles Le Mans for the Formula 1 event. Ridden by Steve Tonkin and George Fogarty, these motors were predecessors of the later 1000cc Le Mans, with 47.5 and 39mm valves. Both machines retired in the race – run under atrocious conditions – with sticking throttle slides. Despite concentrating on preparing Formula 1 Ducatis, Sports Motorcycles continued its involvement with Moto Guzzi in 1978. George Fogarty again rode the Le Mans, but the machine refused to start on the line. After changing a battery, Fogarty got away two minutes late, but soon retired with clutch and transmission problems.

By 1978 the Le Mans was generally outclassed as a racing machine. There were still some entries in the Coupe d'Endurance, and Michel Biver and E Guchet managed 10th place in the Liège 24-hour, with A Rusconi and Giovanni Pretto finishing 8th at Misano.

Stephane Heltal rode the Krajka Le Mans 1000 to 14th place in the 1977 Bol d'Or. (Courtesy Ivar de Gier)

Eddie Roberts
team JAWA
MICHELIN
GEORGE FOGARTY
5
Moto Guzzi
SPORTS MOTOR CYCLES
Lucas
Girling
SPORTS
MOTOR CYCLES
MANCHESTER
CHAMPION
Castrol

Heltal astride the Krajka Le Mans 1000 at the Bol d'Or. (Courtesy Ivar de Gier)

The British Avon production series now required that engines retain their original capacity, disadvantaging the Le Mans against the Laverda 1000cc triple. And whilst Baldwin raced the Le Mans alongside a Ducati in the AMA Superbike Championship, there were no more victories. All twin cylinder machines were suffering as the Japanese improved their fours, and would have to wait until the twins racing series was established to do battle again.

One of the most impressive results was that of the Jan Kampen Guzzi in the 1980 Assen World Championship endurance race, when Theo Louwes finished 10th behind a field of factory four-cylinder machines. Rather than a newer Le Mans, Kampen chose a 1973,

Sports Motorcycles in Manchester entered George Fogarty on its Le Mans, alongside the Ducati of Mike Hailwood, in the 1978 Isle of Man Formula One race. (Courtesy Two Wheels)

black-frame V7 Sport as the basis for this racer. The 850cc engine was from a prototype 850 racer, with the crankshaft and camshaft running in ball bearings, and included every special part that he and Tonti had developed over the years. The gearbox was Kampen's own five-speed design, and one of the unusual features was the pair of BMW constant velocity Bing carburettors. The wheels were specially cast magnesium SMAC from Tony Foale, and the braking system a non-linked, lightened Le Mans system.

When first tested on the short front straight at the Nürburgring, this machine was timed at 230.69kph (144.18mph), the fastest speed ever by a Moto Guzzi at that time. In March 1980, Fred Coopman and Henk Kiewiet rode this machine in the Zandvoort 6-hour race, finishing 14th. Dutch dealer, Theo Louwes, was so impressed that he sponsored the team for the Assen round of the World Endurance Championship in May. This time Coopman and Kiewiet finished 10th, the first private entry behind the Hondas of Fontan and Moineau, and Leon and Chemarin. This final Kampen Guzzi was the last V7 Sport or early Le Mans bike to be successfully raced.

Although the factory had long given up racing the Le Mans, some enthusiastic privateers were still competing in various endurance events. The release of the 850 Le Mans III provided a new basis, and the 1982 season saw a change in fortune for Moto Guzzi in the highly competitive Endurance World Championship. In the opening round at Imola, Francesco Giumbini, Alfio Micheli, and Francesco Tamburini finished 4th, with the German entry of Mattias Meyer and Klaus Hoffman 8th. This was followed by 5th and 9th respectively at the Liège 24-hour race. Giumbini's and Micheli's machine was the final racing Le Mans prepared by Luciano Gazzola and, today, Micheli works as a test rider at Moto Guzzi.

While the 850 Le Mans was generally outclassed in European endurance racing after 1982, several enthusiasts continued to race it with moderate success, including Renato Pasini in Italy and Wolfgang Speyer in Germany. But during 1984, the racing stage shifted to the United States where the Le Mans received a new lease of life as a racing motorcycle.

The Theo Louwes Kampen Guzzi managed an impressive 10th place in the 1980 Assen endurance race. This bike is now owned by Christian de Gier, son of Ivar de Gier. (Courtesy Ivar de Gier)

Racing the V7 Sport and Le Mans

The Transpetrol Le Mans III at the Bol d'Or in 1982. (Courtesy Ivar de Gier)

Dr John Wittner

Release of the Le Mans III provided the impetus for Pennsylvania dentist, Dr John Wittner, to return to racing. Wittner had earlier been a racer and service manager at a Moto Guzzi dealership before training as a dentist. Late in 1983, Wittner approached George A Garbutt at Benelli NA in Baltimore to propose that he prepare a Le Mans III for the 1984 AMA endurance racing series. Under the new rules the 850 Le Mans qualified to compete against 750cc fours in the middleweight category, and by January 1984 a deal was struck with Benelli NA. In the hands of rider, Greg Smrz, the Team Moto Guzzi North America Le Mans III astonished the competition, easily winning the opening race at Rockingham, North Carolina. Ostensibly stock, the success of the Le Mans was due to its incredible reliability (it ran four 6-hour races before requiring a rebuild). Finishing every race, Smrz won the middleweight title, prompting Wittner to sell his dental practice and go racing full-time.

Moto Guzzi provided Wittner with the first Le Mans 1000 to arrive in the United States, and he set about preparing it for the 1985 AMA/CSS US Endurance Road Race Series. Wittner still operated on a shoestring budget out of his workshop in Dowington, Pennsylvania, enlisting support from the Moto Guzzi National Owners' Club. American hot-rod techniques for pushrod V8s were adapted for the pushrod twin, including longer Carillo con-rods (keeping the same stroke), aluminium cylinder plates, and a lightened crankshaft. Cylinder head porting, special, high compression forged pistons, timing gears, new camshaft and valve springs, a stainless steel two-into-one exhaust, and Mikuni carburettors, meant the engine eventually produced 95 horsepower at the rear wheel. While Wittner retained the Le Mans 1000 stock, 16 inch front wheel and 40mm front fork, continual chassis experimentation resulted in much improved handling. As they were now using slick racing tyres that placed more demand on the chassis, Wittner installed a swingarm brace and torque plate connecting the clutch housing to the frame. Racing Koni shocks controlled the rear end, but spring rate, shock length, and spring preload were critical when it came to settling the shaft final drive. The front fork was found to be adequate, although the stock sealed dampers were replaced by conventional racing damper rods. To limit pit stops for fuel in the endurance races a large hump was built in the top of the tank along with a double-dry-break filler system. Knowing the bike would always be at a power disadvantage, Wittner's philosophy was to stay on the track as long as possible, minimising pitstops and concentrating only on being in front at the end of the race.

After solving an early valve gear problem, the team of Greg Smrz and Larry Shorts followed Wittner's orders to a tee. Although not the fastest, the Guzzi was

Speyer on the 850 Le Mans III during 1985. (Courtesy Ivar de Gier)

Dr John Wittner prepared this Le Mans 1000 for the 1985 AMA/CSS US Endurance Road Race series, which Greg Smrz and Larry Shorts convincingly won.

Racing the V7 Sport and Le Mans

the most reliable and economical, eventually winning six races and taking the championship ahead of the new Honda VFR1000, Yamaha FJ1100, and Kawasaki GPz900R. The Dr John Le Mans victory was quite astonishing, receiving considerable publicity as the Daytona endurance race was held the night before a NASCAR race for which many TV crews were present. While everyone was amazed that the venerable air-cooled, two-valve twin could beat the best Japan had to offer in 1985, this was more thanks to the brilliance of Wittner than anything else. He ran the races with a planned scientific strategy, not only calculating how much fuel was required to run a race, but also installing the most powerful lighting system for night riding that the generator could handle.

Although Wittner prepared the Le Mans 1000 for the 1986 season, this year the team struggled financially on limited sponsorship from Benelli North America and the Moto Guzzi National Owners' Club. Wittner found that the Le Mans couldn't compete against the improved Japanese fours, and was plagued with bad luck. After Smrz finished a disappointing seventh in the Battle of the Twins race at Daytona, Wittner decided to enter the Isle of Man TT, but the bike went astray and didn't arrive, ending up in Germany. In July, the team was due to run again at Daytona, receiving one-off sponsorship from Mobil for this event. The race was cancelled after being rained out; the final nail in the coffin for the endurance team.

Drained from several seasons of travelling and endurance racing, Wittner spent the rest of 1986 developing a Battle of the Twins engine, using the endurance chassis as a test bed. A lot more power was needed in order to compete with the Harley-Davidson of Gene Church and Ducati of Jimmy Adamo, and sufficient was eventually coaxed from the two-valve engine. Opening out the bore to 95mm and shortening the stroke to 70mm. the engine was persuaded to rev to 10,500 or sometimes 11,000rpm, but without the impeccable reliability of the endurance motor.

In the meantime, Wittner developed a new frame that would be capable of harnessing this power and went back to Moto Guzzi with plans for a sprint racer for the Battle of the Twins series, which was when events took a turn for the better. De Tomaso was so impressed with Wittner's effort in endurance racing in December 1986 that he flew him to Modena. Wittner showed De Tomaso the chassis plans and he instructed Benelli NA to provide the backing out of its advertising budget. The money was slow to appear but did eventually cover the cost of developing the new frame.

The new frame was very similar to a Tony

With limited sponsorship Wittner struggled in the 1986 Endurance series. (Courtesy Cycle World)

Wittner's Le Mans 1000 was one of the most developed of all two-valve Moto Guzzis. (Courtesy Cycle World)

steering head to a 63mm round steel tube mounted transversely across the swingarm pivot. This tube bolted to 13mm plates cut from aluminium sheet on each side, which also located the swingarm and gearbox. The swingarm employed cantilever rear suspension with a single, Koni F1 car shock absorber. Torque reaction was virtually eliminated with a floating final drive unit pivoting on the axle. Thus, the driveshaft was no longer incorporated in the swingarm and featured

Foale design for Dick Wood of Motomecca, inspired by the Aermacchi Ala d'Oro, although Wittner said his influence came from a Harley Sprint frame built by Jerry Branch for a KR Harley-Davidson in the 1960s. Allegedly five times stronger than the Tonti Guzzi frame, instead of Foale's round spine, Dr John used a strong 50x75mm rectangular section backbone running between the 'V' of the cylinders. Rigidity was ensured by connecting the steering head axis perpendicular to the backbone tube. The backbone, also incorporating the engine breathing system, connected the

an extra, exposed U-joint. To transfer torque reaction from the floating final drive case to a fixed part of the frame was an arm running parallel to the swingarm. This system of a parallel arm working in compression was not unlike the Arturo Magni and Fritz Egli versions.

The Le Mans motor acted as a stressed member, bolted at the front by two triangulated steel tube structures which, in turn, bolted to the backbone tube. These triangulated structures used the upper engine mounts on the timing chest, the lower crankcase mounts being connected by a pair of aluminium plates. The engine was also offset 13mm to the right of the frame to allow for wider racing tyres. The fork rake was 26.5 degrees and the wheelbase 1440mm. It was also important to place the engine as high as was practicable for maximum ground clearance, at the same time keeping the rider low. The spine frame achieved this perfectly with the crankshaft 380mm above the ground and seat height only 770mm. Wheels and brakes were fairly standard racing issue of the period: twin 300mm, fully-floating font discs with four-piston Brembo calipers and Marvic magnesium wheels. While the front was a 17 inch, an 18 inch rear was still employed, and braking was via the hand lever only. A Kelsey-Hayes proportioning valve set the ratio at 90 per cent front and 10 per cent rear. The front fork was a 41.7mm Marzocchi M1R, and the dry weight only 335lb (152kg).

The motorcycle was finished just in time for the Daytona Superbike race in March 1987, at which rider, Doug Brauneck, managed a creditable sixth in the shortened Pro Twins GP race.

For the 1987 Battle of the Twins series the Le Mans engine was further developed. With help from Manfred Hecht of Raceco, Wittner built 17 different motors, some of which didn't survive their first excursion to the redline. Settling on a

For the 1987 Battle of the Twins series, Wittner placed the air-cooled Le Mans engine in a new spine frame with cantilever rear suspension. This was extremely successful and Doug Brauneck won the championship. (Courtesy Two Wheels)

992cc (95.25x70mm) motor, the crankshaft was standard, with Ross pistons machined from forgings intended for small block Chevrolets, and Carillo con-rods. With a set of Mikuni Pro Series power jet, flat slide carburettors, and European Performance Accessories exhaust system, the engine produced around 95 horsepower, but was still extremely fragile and now prone to valve spring failure. Continued development saw the engine eventually produce 102 horsepower at 10,200rpm.

In the second and third Pro Twins race at Road Atlanta and Brainerd, Doug Brauneck finished second, and went into the fourth round with a one point lead over Jimmy Adamo on the Reno Leoni Ducati F1. This time Brauneck proved the Guzzi's superiority, leading from start to finish. Brauneck won again at Road America, and finished second at Laguna Seca after a clutch cable broke. Although he crashed at Mid-Ohio, by the final race at Sears Point Brauneck was comfortably in the lead and his third place finish gave him the championship. It was one of Moto Guzzi's most significant series victories, and provided the company with extraordinary publicity.

Dr John's Battle of the Twins racer was the most successful racing Moto Guzzi since the 1950s. At the beginning of 1988, Wittner took the bike to Italy where it was analysed by factory mechanics for the possibility of installing a four-valve engine in the new chassis. Thus began a new chapter, but the four-valve Daytona never achieved the success of its two-valve brother. Even after Dr John shifted his attention to the new four-valve twin, the two-valve Le Mans lived on for a short while in Battle of the Twins and Classic Twin racing. Chief protagonists were Raceco, headed by Manfred Hecht in America and Amedeo Castellani in the UK. Ian Cobby won the 1989 Classic Bike Champions series on a 950cc Team Clarke/Raceco Le Mans, and Bobby Griffiths piloted Hecht's 992cc, 145kg Le Mans racer to an impressive second in the 1991 Daytona GP2 race.

But no matter how talented and conscientious the tuners, by the end of the 1980s, technology had caught up with the twin cylinder motorcycle. Ducati was showing the way by embracing liquid-cooling and electronic engine management, and in this world the two-valve Le Mans was outclassed. Yet great designs can live longer than they should. Although the Le Mans was not at the technological forefront, Brauneck and Wittner's 1987 Pro Twins championship proved just how competitive the venerable pushrod twin could be.

Appendix

Specifications & production figures

All specifications listed are taken from official publications.

V7 Sport Telaio Rosso 1971 specification

Engine type	Two-cylinder 90 degree four-stroke
Bore	82.5mm
Stroke	70mm
Capacity	748.388cc (45.66cu in)
Compression ratio	9.8:1
Max engine revs	7000rpm
Power	72 horsepower SAE
Valve distribution	Two valves inclined at 70 degrees, driven by a single camshaft with pushrods and rockers
Intake valve	41mm
Exhaust valve	36mm
Valve timing intake opens	40 degrees BTDC
Valve timing intake closes	70 degrees ABDC
Valve timing exhaust opens	63 degrees BBDC
Valve timing exhaust closes	29 degrees ATDC
Valve clearance (cold)	Intake 0.15mm, exhaust 0.20mm
Carburettors	2 Dell'Orto VHB 30 CD and CS with accelerator pumps; choke 30mm, throttle slide 40, atomiser 265, main jet 150, idle jet 50, needle V5 second notch, start atomiser 80, float 10 grams, idle screw $1^{3}/_{4}$ turns out
Ignition	Marelli S311A distributor, 15 degrees static advance, 26 degrees centrifugal, total 40 degrees, points gap 0.42-0.48mm
Sparkplugs	Marelli 225, gap 0.6mm
Starter motor	Bosch 0.4 horsepower
Starter motor crankshaft ratio	1:12 (8/96)
Alternator	Bosch V114-A13 180 watt
Battery	12 volt, 32Ah
Primary gear ratio	16/22 (1.375:1)
First gear	15/27 (1.8:1)
Second gear	19/24 (1.263:1)

Third gear	22/21 (0.954:1)
Fourth gear	24/19 (0.791:1)
Fifth gear	25/17 (0.680:1)
Final drive	8/35 (4.375:1) (optional 9/37 or a 'Sport' 8/37)
Frame	Duplex cradle, tubular CrMo frame with removable lower section
Front fork	35mm telescopic fork with sealed internal damper
Rear suspension	Koni 76F 1267 320mm shock absorbers
Front wheel	Borrani WM2/1.85x18 inch
Rear wheel	Borrani WM3/2.15x18 inch
Front tyre	Michelin 3.25H18 L25 ribbed or S41
Rear tyre	Michelin 3.50x18 S41
Front brake	Twin drum with four leading shoes 220x25mm
Rear brake	Twin leading shoe 220x25mm
Fuel tank	22.5 litres including 3 litres reserve
Wheelbase	1470mm (57.8 inches)
Length	2165mm (85.2 inches)
Width	700mm (27.6 inches)
Height	1035mm (40.7 inches)
Ground clearance	150mm (5.9 inches)
Weight (wet)	225kg (495lb)
Top speed	206kph (129.2mph)
Fuel consumption	8.58 l/100km, 32.8mpg, 27.3mpg (US)

Production V7 Sport specification (differing from Telaio Rosso)

Power	70 horsepower at 7000rpm (53 horsepower at 6300rpm DIN)
Valve clearance (cold)	Intake 0.25mm, exhaust 0.25mm
Carburettors	Main jet 142, needle V9 second notch, idle screw $2\frac{1}{2}$ turns out left carburettor, $2\frac{1}{2}$ to $2\frac{3}{4}$ turns out right carburettor
Ignition	Marelli S311A distributor, 13 degrees static advance, 26 degrees centrifugal, total 39 degrees, points gap 0.37-0.43mm
Sparkplugs	Marelli CW240L, gap 0.6mm or Marelli CW275L, Lodge 4 HLNY; gap 0.5mm (high speed use)
Primary gear ratio	17/21 (1.235:1)
First gear	14/18 (2:1)
Second gear	18/25 (1.388:1)
Third gear	21/22 (1.047:1)
Fourth gear	23/20 (0.869:1)
Fifth gear	24/18 (0.750:1)
Frame	Duplex cradle, tubular steel frame with removable lower section
Front fork	34.7mm telescopic fork with sealed internal damper 0.050 litre Agip F.1 ATF Dexron per leg
Fuel tank	19 litres plus 2 litres reserve
Sump	3.5 litres
Gearbox	0.750 litres
Rear drive	0.360 litres
Acceleration	0-400 metres 13.1 seconds

Production V7 Sport specification, US model from January 1973 (differing from 1972 version)

Power	72 horsepower SAE
Rocker clearance for valve timing	0.6mm (0.23 inch)
Normal rocker clearance (cold)	Inlet and exhaust 0.22mm
Sparkplugs	As before plus Champion N3
Fuel tank	$5\frac{1}{4}$ US gallons including $2\frac{1}{2}$ quarts reserve
Sump	3.5 litres Shell Super 100
Gearbox	0.750 litres Shell Spirax HD 90

Specifications & production figures

Rear drive ... ...0.360 litres Shell Spirax HD 90
Front fork ... ...0.050 litres Shell Tellux 33 per leg
Climbability. ... ...63 per cent in low gear

750 S specification (differing from V7 Sport)
Power ... ...70 horsepower at 7000rpm
Fifth gear 28/21 (0.750:1)
Starter motor... ... ...Bosch DF-12V-0.6 horsepower
Alternator ... ...Bosch G1-14V-20A-21 280 watt
Front brake. ... ...Dual Brembo 300mm disc 15.9mm master cylinder
Fuel tank ... ...22.5 litres (4.1 Imp gallons)
Fuel consumption 8.5 l/100km, 32mpg

750 S3 specification (differing from 750 S)
Power ... ...70 horsepower SAE at 7000rpm
Valve timing intake opens. ... ..20 degrees BTDC
Valve timing intake closes. ... ..52 degrees ABDC
Valve timing exhaust opens... ..52 degrees BBDC
Valve timing exhaust closes .. ..20 degrees ATDC
Final drive... ... ...8/33 (4.714:1)
Front brake. ... ...Twin 300mm disc with 12.7mm master cylinder
Rear brake .. ..242mm disc with 15.875mm master cylinder
Width.. ... ...680mm
Height 1020mm
Curb weight ... ...230kg (206kg dry)
Front fork oil ... ...0.070 litre Agip F1 ATF per leg
Sump. ... ...3.0 litres
Final drive... ... ...0.230 litres Agip F1 Rotra MP SAE 90 plus 0.020 litres of Molykote A
Fuel tank ... ...22 litres
Acceleration ... ...0-400 metres 12.3 seconds
Fuel consumption 6 litres/100km

850 Le Mans 1975-78 specification
Engine type ... ...Two-cylinder 90-degree four-stroke
Bore... ... ...83mm
Stroke 78mm
Capacity. 844cc
Compression ratio... ... .10.2:1
Power ... ...80 horsepower SAE at 7300rpm
Valve distribution. ... ...Two valves inclined at 70 degrees, driven by a single camshaft with pushrods and rockers
Intake valve 44mm
Exhaust valve.. ... ...37mm
Valve timing intake opens. ... ..20 degrees BTDC
Valve timing intake closes. ... ..52 degrees ABDC
Valve timing exhaust opens... ..52 degrees BBDC
Valve timing exhaust closes .. ..20 degrees ATDC
Valve clearance (cold)... ... ..Intake 0.22mm, exhaust 0.22mm
Carburettors ... ...2 Dell'Orto PHF 36 BD and BS with accelerator pumps; choke 36mm, throttle slide 60/1, atomiser 265AB, main jet 135, idle jet 60, needle K5 second notch, start atomiser 70, float 10 grams, idle screw 1½ turns out
Ignition... ... ...8 degrees static advance, 26 degrees centrifugal, total 34 degrees, points gap 0.37-0.43mm
Sparkplugs.. ... ...Bosch 230 T30, Champion N9Y gap 0.5mm
Starter motor... ... ...Bosch DF (L) 12V-0.6 horsepower
Alternator ... ...Bosch G1 (R) 14V 20A 21 (0 120 340 002) 280 watt

Moto Guzzi Sport & Le Mans Bible

Battery	12 V 20Ah
Primary gear ratio	17/21 (1.235:1)
First gear	14/28 (2:1)
Second gear	18/25 (1.388:1)
Third gear	21/22 (1.047:1)
Fourth gear	23/20 (0.869:1)
Fifth gear	28/21 (0.750:1)
Final drive	7/33 (4.714:1)
Frame	Duplex cradle, tubular steel frame with removable lower section
Front fork	34.715mm telescopic fork with sealed internal damper 125mm stroke 0.120 litres Agip F.1 Dexron per leg
Rear suspension	Twin 320mm shock absorbers
Front wheel	FPS aluminium WM3/2.15x18 inch
Rear wheel	FPS aluminium WM3/2.15x18 inch
Front tyre	Metzeler Rille 10 3.50Hx18 or 100/90H18
Rear tyre	Metzeler C7 Block racing 4.10V18, 4.00H18 or 110/90H18
Front brake	Twin drilled 300mm discs with 12.7mm master cylinder
Rear brake	Drilled 242mm disc with 15.875mm master cylinder
Fuel tank	22.5 litres
Wheelbase	1470mm
Length	2190mm
Width	720mm
Height	1030mm
Ground clearance	150mm
Dry weight	198kg (433lb)
Top speed	210kph (130mph)
Fuel consumption	8 litres/100km
Acceleration	400 metres, 11.9 seconds
Sump	3.0 litres Agip SINT 2000 SAE 10W/50
Gearbox	0.750 litres Agip F.1 Rotra MP SAE 90
Final drive	0.230 litres Agip F.1 Rotra MP SAE 90 plus 0.020 litres of Agip Rocol ASO/R

850 Le Mans racing uprating kit part number 14 99 97 40

Camshaft	B10 with 7.2mm intake valve lift
Valve timing intake opens	29 degrees BTDC
Valve timing intake closes	60 degrees ABDC
Valve timing exhaust opens	58 degrees BBDC
Valve timing exhaust closes	31 degrees ATDC
Carburettors	Dell'Orto PHF 40A
Exhaust	Racing megaphone
Primary gear ratio	17/21 (1.235:1), 16/21 (1.312:1)
First gear	17/26 (1.529:1)
Second gear	20/24 (1.200:1)
Third gear	22/22 (1.000:1)
Fourth gear	24/20 (0.833:1)
Fifth gear	25/19 (0.760:1)
Final drive	6/32 (5.333:1), 7/55 (4.714:1), 8/33 (4.125:1), 9/33 (3.778:1)
Fuel tank	24 litre aluminium

Le Mans II 1978-1981 specification (differing from Le Mans)

Maximum torque	7.8kgm at 6600rpm
Carburettors	2 Dell'Orto PHF 36 BD and BS with accelerator pumps; choke 36mm, throttle slide 60/1, atomiser 265AB, main jet 140, idle jet 60, needle K5 second notch, start atomiser 70, float 10 grams, idle screw 1½ turns out
Sparkplugs	Bosch 230 T30, Champion N9Y, lodge 2 HLNY gap 0.5mm

Battery ....12 V 20Ah (12V 32Ah on request)
Front tyre ....Metzeler Rille 10 3.50Hx18 or Pirelli MT 18 100/90H18, or Michelin M45 3.50H18
Rear tyre ....Metzeler C7 Block racing 4.10V18, Michelin M45 4.00H18 or Pirelli MT 18 110/90H18
Wheelbase.. ....1485mm (58.4 inches)
Width.. ....610mm (24 inches)
Height ....1210mm (47 inches)
Ground clearance ....175mm (6.9 inches)
Dry weight 196kg (431lb)
Top speed... ....230kph (144mph)
Fuel consumption 6.5 litres/100km (32mpg)
Front fork ....0.090 litres Agip F.1 ATF Dexron per leg

CX 100 1979 specification (differing from Le Mans II)

Bore... ....88mm
Stroke 78mm
Capacity 948.8cc
Compression ratio.... ....9.2:1
Max torque.. ....8.6 kgm at 5200rpm
Intake valve 41mm
Exhaust valve.. ....36mm
Carburettors ....2 Dell'Orto VHB 30 CD and CS with accelerator pumps; choke 30mm, throttle slide 60, atomiser 265AB, main jet 130, idle jet 50, needle V9 second notch, start atomiser 80
Ignition.... ....2 degrees static advance, 31 degrees centrifugal, total 33 degrees, points gap 0.37-0.43mm
Sparkplugs.. ....Bosch W225 2T, Champion N9Y, AC-44XL, Lodge HLNY, Marelli CW7 LP gap 0.6mm
Starter motor.... ....12V-0.7 KW
Battery ....12 V 20Ah
Dry weight 198kg (433lb)

CX 100 1981 specification (differing from 1979)

Carburettors ....2 Dell'Orto PHF 30 with accelerator pumps; choke 30mm, throttle slide 50/3, atomiser 262AB, main jet 112, idle jet 50, needle K27 second notch, start atomiser 75

Le Mans III 1980-85 specification

Bore... ....83mm
Stroke 78mm
Capacity 844cc
Compression ratio.... ....9.8:1
Maximum torque.. ....7.6kgm at 6,200rpm
Intake valve 44mm
Exhaust valve.. ....37mm
Valve timing intake opens . ...20 degrees BTDC
Valve timing intake closes. ....52 degrees ABDC
Valve timing exhaust opens... ....52 degrees BBDC
Valve timing exhaust closes .. ....20 degrees ATDC
Valve clearance.... ....0.22mm intake and exhaust
Carburettors ....2 Dell'Orto PHF 36 BD and BS with accelerator pumps; choke 36mm, throttle slide 60/3, atomiser 265 AB, main jet 132, (115 USA) idle jet 60 (50 USA), pump jet 33, K18 needle third notch, start atomiser 70, float 10 grams, idle screw 1½ turns out

Ignition	8 degrees static advance, 26 degrees centrifugal, total 34 degrees, points gap 0.37-0.43mm
Sparkplugs	Bosch W5D, Lodge 2 HLHY gap 0.6mm
Starter motor	Bosch 12V-0.7 KW
Alternator	Bosch 14V 20A 280 watt
Battery	12 V 24Ah
Primary gear ratio	17/21 (1.235:1)
First gear	14/28 (2:1)
Second gear	18/25 (1.388:1)
Third gear	21/22 (1.047:1)
Fourth gear	23/20 (0.869:1)
Fifth gear	28/21 (0.750:1)
Final drive	7/33 (4.714:1)
Frame	Duplex cradle, tubular steel frame with removable lower section
Front fork	34.715mm telescopic fork with sealed internal damper 125mm stroke 0.060 litres Agip F.1 Dexron per leg
Rear suspension	Twin 320mm shock absorbers
Front wheel	FPS aluminium WM3/2.15x18 inch CP2
Rear wheel	FPS aluminium WM3/2.15x18 inch CP2
Front tyre	Pirelli 100/90V18
Rear tyre	Pirelli 110/90V18
Front brake	Twin drilled 300mm discs with 12.7mm master cylinder
Rear brake	Drilled 242mm disc with 15.875mm master cylinder
Fuel tank	25 litres
Wheelbase	1,505mm
Length	2190mm
Width	640mm
Height	1160mm
Ground clearance	175mm
Dry weight	20 kg (454lb)
Top speed	230kph (144mph)
Fuel consumption	5.7 litres/100km
Sump	3.0 litres Agip SINT 2000 SAE 10W/50
Gearbox	0.750 litres Agip F.1 Rotra MP SAE 90
Final drive	0.230 litres Agip F.1 Rotra MP SAE 90 plus 0.020 litres of Agip Rocol ASO/R

Le Mans 1000 1984-86 specification

Engine type	Two-cylinder 90 degree four-stroke
Bore	88mm
Stroke	78mm
Capacity	948.8cc
Compression ratio	10:1
Max torque	8.43kgm at 6250rpm
Valve distribution	Two valves inclined at 70 degrees, driven by single camshaft with pushrods and rockers
Intake valve	47mm
Exhaust valve	40mm
Valve timing intake opens	29 degrees BTDC
Valve timing intake closes	60 degrees ABDC
Valve timing exhaust opens	58 degrees BBDC
Valve timing exhaust closes	31 degrees ATDC
Valve clearance (cold)	Intake 0.20mm, exhaust 0.25mm
Carburettors	2 Dell'Orto PHM 40 ND and NS with accelerator pumps; choke 40mm, throttle slide 60/5 (50/3 USA), atomiser 268AB (260 USA), main jet 145 (150 USA), idle jet 57 (62 USA), needle K19 (K33 USA) third notch, start

Specifications & Production Figures

Ignition	atomiser 60, float 10 grams, idle screw 1½ turns out 8 degrees static advance, 26 degrees centrifugal, total 34 degrees, points gap 0.37-0.43mm
Sparkplugs	Bosch W5 DC gap 0.6mm
Starter motor	12V-0.7 KW
Alternator	14V 20A 280 watt
Battery	12 V 24Ah Fiamm 61 130P
Primary gear ratio	17/21 (1.235:1)
First gear	14/28 (2:1)
Second gear	18/25 (1.388:1)
Third gear	21/22 (1.047:1)
Fourth gear	23/20 (0.869:1)
Fifth gear	28/21 (0.750:1)
Final drive	7/33 (4.714:1)
Frame	Duplex cradle, tubular steel frame with removable lower section
Front fork	40mm telescopic fork with sealed internal damper and dual springs 140mm stroke 0.150 litres Agip F.1 Dexron per leg
Rear suspension	Twin Koni 337mm shock absorbers
Front wheel	Aluminium 16 MT 2.50 H2
Rear wheel	Aluminium 18 MT 3.00 H2
Front tyre	120/80 V16 tube or tubeless
Rear tyre	130/80 V18 tube or tubeless
Front brake	Twin drilled 270mm discs with 12.7mm master cylinder
Rear brake	Drilled 270mm disc with 15.875mm master cylinder
Fuel tank	24 litres
Wheelbase	1514mm
Length	2160mm
Width	680mm
Height	1,220mm
Ground clearance	120mm
Dry weight	215kg (474lb)
Top speed	230kph (143mph)
Fuel consumption	5.4 litres/100km
Sump	3.0 litres Agip SINT 2000 SAE 10W/50
Gearbox	0.750 litres Agip F.1 Rotra MP SAE 90
Final drive	0.230 litres Agip F.1 Rotra MP SAE 90 plus 0.020 litres of Agip Rocol ASO/R

Le Mans 1000 SE specification 1986 (differing from Le Mans 1000)

Primary gear ratio	18/23 (1.277:1)
First gear	17/28 (1.647:1)
Second gear	21/24 (1.142:1)
Third gear	23/21 (0.913:1)
Fourth gear	25/19 (0.760:1)
Fifth gear	27/19 (0.704:1)
Final drive	7/33 (4.714:1)
Front tyre	120/80 VR16 Pirelli MP7R radial
Rear tyre	130/80 VR18 Pirelli MP7R radial
Wheelbase	1485mm

Le Mans 1000 CI 1988-93 specification (differing from Le Mans 1000)

Battery	12V 23Ah Tudor 6M 034
Front fork	40mm
Rear suspension	Twin Koni 337mm shock absorbers
Front wheel	Aluminium 18 MT 2.50 H2
Rear wheel	Aluminium 18 MT 3.00 H2

Moto Guzzi Sport & Le Mans Bible

Front tyre	100/90 V10 tube or tubeless
Rear tyre	120/90 V18 tube or tubeless
Front brake	13mm master cylinder
Fuel tank	25 litres
Wheelbase	1485mm
Length	2180mm
Width	740mm

1000 S/SE 1990-91 specification (differing from Le Mans 1000 CI)

Carburettors	2 Dell'Orto PHM 40 ND and NS atomiser 266AB (all other jetting unchanged)
Fork rake and trail	62 degrees and 106mm
Front fork	0.070 litres Agip ATF Dexron per leg
Fork travel	140mm
Shock absorber travel	75mm
Length	2200mm
Width	720mm
Height	1260mm
Seat height	780mm
Ground clearance	160mm
Fuel tank	24 litres
Dry weight	215kg (475lb), (218kg SE)
Top speed	230kph (144mph)
Fuel consumption	5.4 litres/100km (53mpg, 44mpg US)

1000 S 1992-93 specification (differing from 1000 S 1990-91)

Compression ratio	9.5:1
Max power	71 horsepower at 6800rpm
Max torque	7.9kgm at 5800rpm
Intake valve	44mm
Exhaust valve	37mm
Valve clearance (cold)	0.22mm intake and exhaust
Carburettors	2 Dell'Orto PHF 36 DD and DS with accelerator pumps; choke 36mm, throttle slide 60/3 (50/3 USA), atomiser 268AB (261 USA), main jet 130 (130 USA), idle jet 50 (48 USA), needle K18 (K27 USA) third notch, start atomiser 70, float 8.5 grams
Ignition	Motoplat electronic 2-3 degrees static advance, 34-35 maximum, rotor gap 0.2-0.4mm (Magneti Marelli Digiplex preset from 1993)
Sparkplugs	Bosch W5DC, NGK BP 7ES, Champion N9YC gap 0.6mm; Bosch W7DC, NGK BP 6ES gap 0.7mm (Digiplex)
Starter motor	Valeo 12V 1.2 KW
Alternator	14V 25A 350 Watt Ducati
Battery	12V 24Ah Fiamm 61F 130P, AAA 6PLH; 12V 28Ah Varta 52 816PS

Production data V7 Sport, 750 S, and 750 S3

Model	1971	1972	1973	1974	1975	Total
V7 Sport drum	104	2152	1435		100	3791
V7 Sport USA disc brake			152			152
V750 S EU disc brake				948		948
750 S3 IT/EU					950	950
Total	104	2152	1587	948	1050	5841

Specifications & production figures

Production data Le Mans, Le Mans II, 1000 CX

Model	1975	1976	1977	1978	1979	1980	1981	Total
Le Mans	219	2532	2548	1737				7036
Le Mans II				560	2980	2786	1009	7335
100 CX US					281		72	353
Total	219	2532	2548	2297	3261	2786	1081	14,724

Production data 850 Le Mans III, Le Mans 1000

Model	1980	1981	1982	1983	1984	1985	1986	1987	1988	Total
Le Mans III	180	2296	3288	2609	1625	58				10,056
1000 Le Mans					460	1766	1179	754	71	4230
Total	180	2296	3288	2609	2085	1824	1179	754	71	14,286

Production data Le Mans CI, 1000 S

Model	1988	1989	1990	1991	1992	1993	Total
1000 Le Mans CI	724	720	325	147	143	54	2113
1000 S		155	524	401	196	84	1360
Total	724	875	849	548	339	138	3473

Also from Veloce –

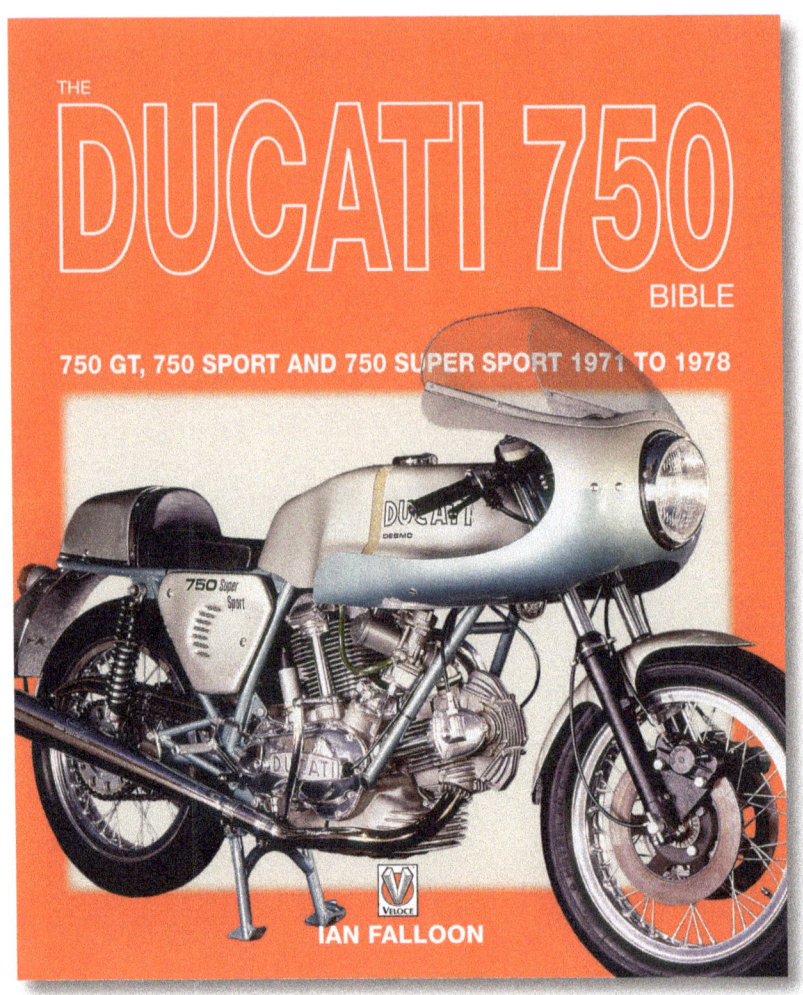

When the great Ducati engineer Fabio Taglioni designed the 750 Ducati in 1970 there was no way he could comprehend how important this model would be. The 750, the Formula 750 racer and the Super Sport became legend: this book celebrates these machines. Year-by-year, model-by-model, change-by-change detail.

ISBN: 978-1-845840-12-9
Hardback • 25x20.7cm • 160 pages • 163 colour and b&w pictures

For more info on Veloce titles, visit our website at www.veloce.co.uk
• email: info@veloce.co.uk • Tel: +44(0)1305 260068

Also from Veloce –

This book covers all of the landmark square-case Ducatis of the 1970s and 1980s, including the 900 Super Sport and the Mike Hailwood Replica. Illustrated with 200 pictures, and incorporating complete appendices of technical specifications, this book is a must-have for any lover of fine motorcycles.

ISBN: 978-1-84584-121-8
Hardback • 25x20.7cm • 160 pages • 178 colour and b&w pictures

For more info on Veloce titles, visit our website at www.veloce.co.uk
• email: info@veloce.co.uk • Tel: +44(0)1305 260068

Also from Veloce –

Although manufactured for only one year – 1974 – the Ducati 750 Super Sport was immediately touted as a future classic. It was a pioneer motorcycle – expensive and rare, and produced by Ducati's race department to celebrate victory in the 1972 Imola 200 Formula 750 race.
Owing to its uniqueness and rarity, the 750 SS has become extremely valuable and desirable, fetching prices beyond the most expensive contemporary Ducati; for Ducatisti, it is the Holy Grail.

ISBN: 978-1-84584-202-4
Hardback • 25x25cm • 176 pages • 259 colour and b&w pictures

For more info on Veloce titles, visit our website at www.veloce.co.uk
• email: info@veloce.co.uk • Tel: +44(0)1305 260068

Also from Veloce –

The overhead camshaft single provided the DNA for Ducati motorcycles, but, with little accurate documentation and information available until now, they can be difficult to restore and authenticate. This is the first book to provide an authoritative description of the complete range of Ducati OHC singles.

ISBN: 978-1-845845-66-7
Hardback • 25x25cm • 288 pages • 715 colour pictures

For more info on Veloce titles, visit our website at www.veloce.co.uk
• email: info@veloce.co.uk • Tel: +44(0)1305 260068

Also from Veloce –

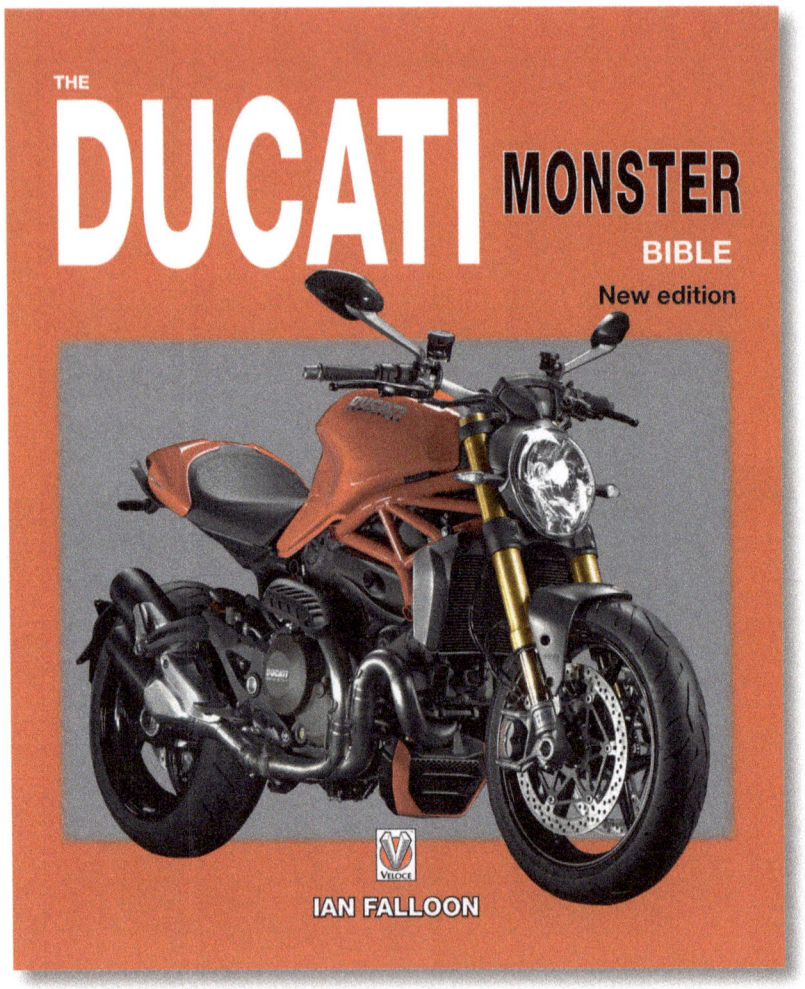

When Ducati released the Monster in 1993 it created a new niche market for the naked motorcycle that continues today. Continual advancement over the past 20 years has enhanced the Monster's 'less-is-more' philosophy, and Ducati has created Monsters to suit everyone, from entry-level 400s and 600s to 1100cc superbikes. All Monsters share the naked style that showcases the engine and chassis, and provide superb handling suitable for cities or canyons.

ISBN: 978-1-84584616-9
Hardback • 25x20.7cm • 176 pages • 197 colour pictures

For more info on Veloce titles, visit our website at www.veloce.co.uk
• email: info@veloce.co.uk • Tel: +44(0)1305 260068

Index

A&G Motorrad 119, 121
Abarth 13
Adamo, Jimmy 141, 144
Aermacchi 14, 19, 142
Agostini, Duilio 11, 132, 134
Agostini, Giacomo 63
AJS 10
Alberici 20
Alfa Romeo 12
AMA 125, 126, 132
AMA Superbike Championship 132, 134, 137
AMA/CCS US Endurance Series 139-142
America 85, 135, 144
Amsterdam Show (RAI) 118, 119
Anderson, Fergus 10, 11,
Argentina 38
Armstrong, Roy 135
Assen 137, 138
Auerbacher, George 14
Australia 97
Avon Roadrunner Production Series 135, 137
Axtell, C R 125

Baldwin, Mike 134, 135, 137
Baltimore 121, 139
Barcelona 7, 135
Barcelona 24-hour race 60, 129
Barrett 42
Barrington, Manliff 10
Battle of the Twins 141, 143, 144
Benelli 14, 17, 38, 46, 50, 59, 60, 62, 66
Benelli North America 94, 139, 141
Benelux 119
Berliner 14, 17, 29, 35, 42, 50, 81
Bertarelli, Silvano 14
Bertorello 129
Bianchi 14, 19
Bike magazine 55, 69, 123
Biotti, Alcide 19
Biver, Michel 135
Blair, Bob 125
Blegi 127
BMW 9, 12, 56, 66, 75, 134
Bol d'Or 60, 62, 66, 125-127, 129, 132, 134, 135, 137, 139
Bologna 54
Bonalumi 127
Botta, Francesco 19
Brainerd 144
Brambilla, Ernesto 129
Brambilla, Vittorio 14, 127, 129
Brauneck, Doug 143, 144
Brettoni, Augusto 127

Britain 29, 56
British market 81
BSA 127
Butler & Smith 134

California 126
Campbell, Keith 12
Cann, Maurice 10,
Carcano, Giulio Cesare 9-13,
Carena 129
Casadio, Ettore 15, 127
Castellani, Amedeo 144
Cattaneo, Donato 14
Cavalli 129
Cecere, Maurizio 128, 129
Cereda 129
Charlotte, North Carolina 134
Chemarin 138
Church, Gene 141
Classic Twin racing 144
Cobby, Ian 144
Coburn & Hughes 56, 81, 94
Coopman, Fred 138
Coupe d'Endurance 132, 135
Cretti, Bruno 127
Cycle magazine 29, 83, 94, 104

D'Angelo 135
Dale, Dickie 11, 12
Daytona 125, 134, 135, 141, 143, 144
De Gier, Christian 138
De Gier, Ivar 12, 13, 20, 22, 23, 29, 47, 52, 59, 89, 116, 118, 119, 126
De Stefani, Romolo 14, 19
De Tomaso, Alejandro 38, 46, 47, 52, 53, 59, 60, 62, 72, 73, 75, 77, 79, 86, 94, 97, 119, 129, 141
Delft, University of 59, 126
Donghi, Paolo 119
Dorset 104
Dowington, Pennsylvania 139
Ducati 13, 17, 23, 26, 29, 35, 42, 50, 56, 66, 69, 76, 81, 97, 99, 114, 118, 125, 129, 132, 134, 137, 141, 144
Dutch production championship 126

Egli, Fritz 143
Endurance World Championship 137, 138
Ethiopia 8
Europe 86, 121, 123, 124
European Championship 7

Fascist government 8
Fiat 12, 13, 126
FIM 19, 21, 135

Findlay, Jack 129, 130
Fittipaldi, Emerson 23
FMI 52
Foale, Tony 138, 142
Fogarty, George 135, 137
Fontan 138
Formula One car racing 23
France 50

Galtrucco 127
Garbutt, George A 94, 139
Gazzola, Luciano 14, 15, 17, 19, 21-23, 29, 31, 61, 62, 66, 73, 127, 129, 131-134, 138
Genoa 7
Germany 20, 50, 79, 97, 138, 141
Gianini, Carlo 10
Gilera 9, 11-14
Giugiaro, Giorgetto 50
Giumbini, Francesco 138
Greenib 119
Griffiths, Bobby 144
Gritti, Alessandro 125
Guchet, E 137
Guzzi, Carlo 6-9

Hailwood, Mike 19-21, 129, 137
Harley-Davidson 66, 125, 141, 142
Hecht, Manfred 144
Heltal, Stephane 135, 137
Hoffman, Klaus 138
Holland 59, 63, 102
Honda 33, 50, 59, 114, 118, 127, 138, 141

Ickx, Jacky 23
IMI 17, 22
Imola 52, 129-131, 138
Imola Gold Cup 12
Innocenti 86
Isle of Man TT and F1 7, 8, 10, 11, 135, 137, 141
Ital Design 50
Italian Championships 6, 129, 132
Italian Ministry of Transport 25
Italy 20, 138, 144

Japan 141

Kampen, Jan 15, 19, 59, 63, 126, 132, 137, 138
Kavanagh, Ken 10, 11
Kawasaki 33, 56, 141
Kerker, George 15, 29, 125
Kiewiet, Henk 138
Klaver, Paul 59

Krajka, Charles 125, 126, 135, 137

La Moto magazine 63
Laguna Seca 134, 144
Lake Como 6, 19
Laverda 13, 15, 17, 26, 29, 35, 42, 50, 56, 69, 97, 99, 127, 129, 132, 137
Lawrence of Arabia 38
Le Mans 127
Leon 138
Leoni, Reno 132, 134, 135, 144
Letto di Priolo, Dore 19
Leytonstone 28
Liebmann, Kurt 134
Liège 129, 137, 138
Lillington, North Carolina 121
Linto 14, 19
Lomas, Bill 11, 12
Lorenzetti, Enrico 10
Loudon 134
Louwes, Theo 138
Luton 94

Macchi, Orlando 132
Magni, Arturo 143
Mambretti 127
Manchester 135, 137
Mandello del Lario 6, 17, 25, 59, 60, 75, 86, 125
Mandracci, Guido 14, 127, 129
Marcantonio, Arnaldo 17
Maserati 94, 121
Mentasti, Guido 7
Meyer, Mattias 138
Micheli, Alfio 138
Micucci, Antonio 13, 16
Mid Ohio 144
Milan 6, 12, 22, 26, 54, 86
Milan Show 20, 21, 47, 62
Misano 132
Modena 59, 86, 127-129, 141
Moineau 138
Mondial 12, 14
Montanari, Alano 10
Montjuich 60, 132
Montlhèry 125
Monza 7, 14, 18-20, 34, 125-127, 129-132
Morante 135
Moto America 121
Moto Guzzi National Owners Club 139, 141
Motobecane 97
Motociclismo magazine 33, 79, 92, 104
Motogiro 125
Motomecca 142
Motor Cycle 7, 55
Motor Cycle Mechanics 29
Motor Cycle News 29, 69
Motorcycle Sport 29

Motorcyclist magazine 108
Mugello 132
Mulazzani 129, 132
Mussolini 8
MV Agusta 11, 17, 23, 67
NASCAR 141
Netherlands 50, 119, 126
Norton 7, 10, 15, 50, 66, 126, 127
NSU 9, 12
Nürburgring 138

Ozzano Emilia 32

Pagani, Alberto 14
Parodi, Emanuele Vittorio 7
Parodi, Enrico 9, 11, 12
Parodi, Giorgio 6, 9
Pasini, Renato 138
Paton 14, 19
Patrignani, Roberto 14
Pennsylvania 139
Performance Bikes magazine 114
Pesaro 59
Peugeot 7
Piazzalunga, Pierantonio 127
Pickrell, Ray 127
Pinifarina 75
Pocono 134
Pontedera 24
Premier Motor Corporation 35, 132
Premio Varrone 60, 61
Pretto, Giovanni 137
Pro-Twins GP Races 143, 144

Raceco 144
Ravelli, Giovanni 6
Redhill 42
Riva, Raimondo 15, 127, 129, 132
Rivetts 28, 29
Road America 144
Road Atlanta 144
Rockingham, North Carolina 139
Rollo, Abrama 127
Romeri 132
Rossi, Luciano 15, 125
Rubio, Perez 135
Ruffo, Bruno 10
Rusconi, A 137

Sarolea 7
Sciaresa, Abbondio 127, 129, 132, 133
Scola, Bruno 17, 132, 134, 135
Sear, John 135
Sears Point 144
Second World War 7
SEIMM 14, 38
Shorts, Larry 140, 141
Smrz, Greg 139-141
Societè Anomina Moto Guzzi 7

Soldavini 13
Spain 27
Speyer, Wolfgang 138, 139
Sports Motorcycles 135, 137
Stevens, Peter 97
Sunbeam 7
Surrey 42
Suzuki 118
Sydney Opera House 107

Tait, Percy 127
Tamburini, Francesco 138
Tavernese 128
Team Moto Guzzi North America 139
Tenconi, Angelo 14
Tengali 24
Tenni, Omobono 8
Texas 126
Three Cross Motorcycles 104, 121
Todero, Umberto 13, 23, 54, 89
Toè Giuseppe Dal 14
Tonkin, Steve 135
Tonti, Lino 14, 17-20, 22, 23, 25, 28, 29, 47, 50, 52, 54, 59, 60, 75, 86, 89, 111, 125-127, 132, 138
Tonzanico 6, 7
Trabalzini, Franco 14
Triumph 15, 50, 125, 127, 129
Trofeo La Moto 1000 132, 133
Tuscany 24
TüV 54

UK 28, 42, 50, 56, 75, 79, 82, 94, 104, 115, 118, 121
US (USA) 14, 17, 30, 35-40, 50, 52, 63, 81, 85, 92, 94, 100, 104, 107, 116, 118, 121, 123-125, 139

Valentini, Sergio 127
Vallelunga 127-129, 132
Venturi, Remo 14, 15
Voghera 21
Volkswagen 59, 126

Wall Street Crash 8,
Warmond 119
Wittner, Dr John 139-142, 144
Wood, Dick 142
Woods, Stanley 7, 8
World Championships 6, 10, 12, 138

Yamaha 118, 141

Zandvoort 59, 126, 138
ZDS 125-126
Zolder 129

www.ingramcontent.com/pod-product-compliance
Lightning Source LLC
Chambersburg PA
CBHW061748290426
44108CB00028B/2927